WHY THE

MYSTICS MATTER NOW

WHY THE
MYSTICS MATTER
NOW

THOMAS MERTON

THÉRÈSE OF LISIEUX

HILDEGARD OF BINGEN

JULIAN OF NORWICH

MEISTER ECKHART

IGNATIUS OF LOYOLA

CATHERINE OF SIENA

FREDERICK BAUERSCHMIDT

SORIN BOOKS   Notre Dame, Indiana

www.sorinbooks.com

International Standard Book Number: 1-893732-71-1

Cover design by Eyecreate/Bill Ferguson

Text design by Brian C. Conley

Printed and bound in the United States of America.

Library of Congress Cataloging-in-Publication Data
Bauerschmidt, Frederick Christian.
      Why the mystics matter now / Frederick Bauerschmidt.
         p. cm.
      ISBN 1-893732-71-1 (pbk.)
      1. Mysticism--Catholic Church--History. 2. Spiritual life--Catholic Church. 3. Mystics--History. I. Title.

      BV5082.3.B38 2003
      248.2'2--dc21

                        2003007141

Contents

Introduction

WHAT ARE MYSTICS AND WHY DO THEY MATTER?

Let me be perfectly honest at the outset: I am not exactly sure what a mystic is. The words "mystic" and "mystical" and "mysticism" seem to have as many meanings as there are people who use the words. If we move from explicit meanings to the associations that these words arouse, the matter seems even more confusing. My word processor's thesaurus gives the following synonyms for "mysticism": cabalism, occult, supernatural, hocus-pocus, magic, necromancy, sorcery, voodoo, witchcraft. Such a list seems to point us in the direction of Harry Potter or *The X-Files*, not any genuine spiritual tradition. I am tempted to conclude that the words have become so vague and misleading that we should simply discard them.

Such a conclusion may seem sensible, but words are notoriously difficult to take out of circulation by decree. The fact is, despite the deep confusion and obscurity that accompanies these terms, some people get described as "mystics," some phenomena are described as "mystical," and these people and phenomena together are spoken of as embodying "mysticism." It would involve as much effort to avoid the use of these terms as it would be to define them in some precise way. What I hope to do in this introduction is to give some idea of why these terms remain useful and what they might mean, as well as to make clear how I will be using them in reference to the Christian mystical tradition. I hope that in beginning to see what a mystic is, we will already be beginning to see why they matter.

MYSTICISM AND EXPERIENCE

One use of the term mystic is to refer to someone who has experienced an altered state of consciousness that has brought them to a new awareness of ultimate reality. Such a definition casts the mystical net as widely as possible, seeking to include members of all religions, and even those who do not practice what we would normally think of as a religion. In this view, above and even apart from the particulars of religion, there is an experience of unity with or awareness of some sort of ultimate reality that transcends and unites all religions. The Buddhist sage, the Sufi *shaykh*, the rabbi who practices Kabbalah, the Christian visionary, the person of no religion who looks upon the ocean and feels a connection with all reality—all of these have the same transcendental mystical experience, though they articulate it in the languages of their different belief systems. Mysticism names what they all share, despite their religious differences.

This use of the language of mysticism has obvious appeals. It offers an account of why people in different religious traditions report similar experiences of being taken out of their normal way of looking at things and acquiring a new way of looking at things. It also holds out the hope that, rather than being the divisive force that it has often been in history, religion can become a profound source of unity, if we focus on its mystical core.

At the same time, this use of the language of mysticism has some obvious problems. A deeper probing of the reports of these seemingly similar experiences often reveal the similarities to be more superficial than deep. Both the Buddhist sage and the Christian visionary may speak of an experience of unity with ultimate reality, but it is not clear that they mean the same thing either by unity or reality. The Buddhist may mean a unity that obliterates all difference, while the Christian might mean the unity of love, which depends upon the distinction of lover and beloved; the Buddhist might mean an ultimate reality of emptiness, while a Christian might mean God. Likewise, in seeking to describe another religion in terms of its mystical core, there is always the danger that one religion is simply redescribing another religion in its own terms. Christians have a notorious difficulty in doing justice to the radical nondualism of Buddhism, and Buddhist redescriptions of Christian love in terms of universal compassion also seem to miss something vital. In other words, we must always be aware that different religious traditions might simply be different, in both their methods and their goals, and we might need to live with and even honor that difference without redescribing it in terms of sameness.

Mystical Traditions

The alternative approach is to try to speak of mysticism from within a particular tradition. Here matters become a bit easier, since the vocabulary used is embedded in traditions and practices that give the terms a somewhat more stable meaning. The Zen

Buddhist practice of "sitting meditation" is inseparable from the "nonclinging" state of consciousness that Zen seeks to uncover. Christian meditation on Biblical books such as The Song of Songs is integrally related to the union in love with the Triune God that is the goal of all Christian life. In this second approach, we make no attempts to find a perspective outside these particular traditions of practice from which we might observe them and say that they are seeking the same thing. What we do is to explore deeply the dynamics of a particular tradition. This requires the attempt to understand this tradition from within.

Such an approach might make it sound as if religious traditions are completely sealed off from each other, with nothing to say to each other and nothing to hear. But this is absolutely not the case; no religion is an island, and interactions between religious traditions happen all the time. Sometimes these interactions are violent, involving rejection of the other. But sometimes they are helpful and fruitful interactions, in which one recognizes truth in another tradition.

The medieval Christian theologian Thomas Aquinas immersed himself in the writings of the pagan Aristotle, the Muslim Ibn Sina, and the Jew Moses Maimonides so that he could be a better theologian. He did not have a theory of how it was possible for him to do this, apart from the conviction that all truth comes from the one God who made the world (a conviction that some of his dialogue partners did not share); he simply did it. The same thing happens with mystical traditions. One of the most important figures of

Christian mysticism, the fifth-century Syrian monk known as Dionysus the Areopagite, was heavily influenced by pagan neoplatonism, and various sixteenth-century Christian writers drew on Jewish Kabbalistic and Islamic Sufi writings. In a writer like the Trappist monk Thomas Merton, the influences are obvious, particularly the influences from Zen Buddhism. Zen itself arises from the influence of Taoism and Confucianism on Mahayana Buddhism. Although these borrowings by figures in a particular tradition sometimes lead others in that tradition to look upon them suspiciously, it is clear that Christians like Merton and Dionysius, or Buddhists who practice Zen, remain recognizably within their traditions.

Traditions are living things, and therefore admit to a certain flexibility. One does not need a theory that says that all religions share a "mystical core" in order to recognize that different traditions can learn from each other. In fact, one does not need any sort of theory at all. One simply needs a grounding in one's own tradition, an openness to another tradition, and a willingness to do the hard work of learning.

From a Christian Perspective

This is a book about the Christian mystical tradition, written by a Christian. But I have tried to write both for those who are Christians and for those who are not. My experience is that I have learned things from non-Christians that have helped me to be a better Christian. I do not have a theory about how this is possible, nor do I feel the need for one. I simply know that it has happened. And in light of this experience, I hope that I can write something that will not only be of benefit to Christians, but to non-Christians as well.

Writing as a Christian about the Christian mystical tradition, I think it is important not to strip away all that is particular to Christianity. Such stripping away is less like shucking corn and more like peeling an onion. One might need to break through the papery, outer covering in order to let the juices flow, but if you keep on peeling, you will soon have nothing left. In describing the tradition of Christian mysticism, one simply cannot avoid mentioning Jesus Christ and the saints and the scriptures and the sacraments, since these are the lifeblood of this tradition. At the same time, it is impossible to say beforehand that someone who does not share Christian convictions about Jesus or the Bible will have nothing to learn from encountering this tradition. Much will depend on the openness of the reader, and on my own ability to say why I think the figures we look at matter today.

THE LANGUAGE OF MYSTERY

If we look at the use of the language of "mysticism" within the particular religious tradition of Christianity, we can begin to sketch out some common features of those who are referred to as "mystics." In early Christian usage, the adjective mystical (there were at this point no words corresponding to the nouns mystic and mysticism) was closely related to the term mystery, both of them deriving from the Greek root word *mu*, meaning to close or to hide. The language of mystery is common in the writings of Paul in the New Testament (e.g., Romans 16:25, 1 Corinthians 2:1, Ephesians 3:3–9,

Colossians 1:26–27, 1 Timothy 3:16), where it usually refers to God's plan to redeem the world through the life, death, and resurrection of Jesus, a mystery that is now openly proclaimed by Paul, but yet somehow remains mysterious. The word mystical does not occur in the Bible at all, but it is found in other early Christian writings to describe the means by which believers come to share in the salvation brought by Jesus. The two most common contexts in which we find the word mystical used in the first centuries of Christianity are those of interpretation of the Bible and the celebration of those rituals that came to be called mysteries or sacraments. A brief look at these two contexts can help us to begin to define what mystical might mean in a Christian context.

In the Christian tradition the writings of the Bible, and especially the Psalms, have been key texts for prayer. But these texts have presented certain difficulties. For example, when Psalm 137, speaking to the "daughter of Babylon," says, "happy shall they be who take your little ones and dash them against the rock!" it seems to commend the infanticide of Babylonian babies. But not only were such actions not in keeping with the teachings of Jesus, they were also not very edifying for prayer. So Christians took this passage not as a recommendation for genocide, but as a veiled statement about how we should care for our souls, rooting out at the very start the evil thoughts (the "little ones" of Babylon) and breaking them against the "rock," which is Christ. The profound experience of salvation through Jesus led the early Christians to read the whole Bible, the Old Testament as well as the New, as being about Christ. So in Psalm 137, "the rock" become Jesus Christ, the sure foundation of our souls.

This practice of looking beyond the veil of the surface meaning of a text to a deeper and hidden meaning came to be called mystical interpretation. This deeper meaning might have to do with shaping our moral lives, or it may have to do with the new covenant of Jesus Christ being "hidden" in the old covenant with Israel. Since this practice grew out of using the biblical text for prayer, it was those whose prayer lives had the greatest depths who were held to be the best interpreters of the Bible. Thus the "mystical interpretation" of the Bible was intertwined with the life of prayer, and it was through the practice of such interpretation that one came into living contact with the living God.

UNVEILING REALITY

Scriptural interpretation was crucial for early Christianity, but Christians were not simply "people of the book." They were also people who engaged in certain ritual actions that they believed brought them into union with God. To an outside observer, these rituals seemed quite ordinary: washing, eating, marrying, anointing the sick (a common medical procedure in the ancient world). Christians, however, held that these actions had a deeper significance. Just as there were hidden depths of meaning in the words and events of the Bible, so too in these actions—which the early Christians called mysteries—there was a hidden reservoir of meaning. The bath that Christians called Baptism was a mystical washing of sins. The meal that

Christians called the Eucharist (thanksgiving) was a mystical meal in which bread became Christ's mystical body.

It will only be later that the adjective mystical comes to have the connotation of unreal. For the early Christians, when they said that baptism was a mystical washing, they did not mean that it was not a *real* washing; indeed, it was the *most* real washing possible, the washing away of sin. The mystical body that Christians received in their Eucharistic meal was not *less* real for being mystical; it was *more* real. One of the most poetic and profound early Christian writers, Ephrem the Syrian, wrote of the Eucharist: "the Spirit is in your Bread, the Fire in your Wine, a manifest wonder, that our lips have received." But the realities brought about in the celebration of these mysteries was not a "manifest wonder" to the eye of the disinterested observer. Just as with the interpretation of scripture, the significance of the sacramental mysteries is veiled, and can be seen best by one who immerses herself in the life of prayer, for it is prayer that opens for us these previously hidden aspects of reality.

FOR ALL TO EXPERIENCE

But so far I haven't really gotten to the question, "Who are the mystics?" and this is because for most of its history Christianity has resisted the idea that there is a special class of people who have a special experience of God that is somehow unavailable to "normal" people. The terms "mystic" and "mysticism," which seem to denote distinct kinds of people and experiences, do not come into common use until the sixteenth and seventeenth centuries. Prior to this the adjective "mystical" was used to describe a certain depth of experience of God, but it was the same experience of God that was had by all Christians. All Christians encountered God in scripture and sacrament. All had the mystery of Christ revealed to them in the Bible. All received the mystical washing of Baptism and shared in the mystical meal of the Eucharist.

At the same time, there was (and continues to be) a certain hiddenness or depth to both scripture and sacrament, a depth that can be found through a life dedicated to prayer. Drawing on certain philosophical ideals from the ancient world, this life of prayer came to be known as the contemplative life. This was a life that was oriented above all to discernment of and meditation upon the mystery of God, often lived in a community of others dedicated to that same life. In devoting time to private and communal prayer, the men and women who lived the contemplative life did not see themselves as pursuing something different from ordinary Christians; they simply sought to plumb more deeply the ordinary mysteries of scripture and sacrament. And it is the writings of these men and women that make up much of what we might call the Christian mystical tradition.

This book does not attempt to be a comprehensive account of this tradition, and many figures are omitted. Some may wonder why monumental figures like Teresa of Avila or John of the Cross are not included, or why Eastern Christian or Protestant writers are not included. Inclusions and omissions have been dictated almost entirely by my own abilities or lack of abilities. I have chosen figures about whom I know something and whom I judge to be particularly helpful in looking at a specific issue. This book is certainly not the last word on why the mystics matter; my only hope is that for some it might be a first.

EMBARKING ON A JOURNEY

In the writings of the mystical or contemplative tradition, certain common themes recur. One particularly common one is what we might call the three-fold journey to God. Drawing on their own experience of the contemplative life, these writers note three phases or stages that people commonly pass through in seeking to know the mysteries of God more deeply.

The first of these is *purgation* or *purification*. On one level, this is a purification from sin or, put more positively, a purification of desire. In this phase, one seeks to reorient one's desires toward God, the ultimate goodness. This means turning away from the partially good things of this world or, again put more positively, coming to see their goodness as sharing in the infinite goodness of God. This is an arduous phase in which one must constantly seek God's help in prayer.

The second stage or phase is *illumination*, in which one's mind is flooded by divine light. This can take many forms. In some rare cases people receive visions or hear voices; more commonly one will experience joy and delight in prayer, have a clearer insight into the mysteries of faith, or simply have a profound feeling of peace. Yet mystical writers warn that these experiences can be dangerously misleading, particularly the more exotic ones like visions. They can be dangerous because we can mistake our experience of God for the reality of God, and we presume that when we are not experiencing joy or delight or peace that God is not there. We come to worship our experiences rather than God. So there must be a constant return to the stage of purification, only this time we are not purged of our disordered love for worldly things, but of our disordered love for spiritual things. Thus much of the contemplative life involves something of an alternation between purification and illumination.

The third stage or phase of the contemplative life is *union*. Here one reaches beyond one's own ideas about and experiences of God to enter the presence of the living God. Unlike the experiences associated with illumination, this is not a discrete event that one experiences, rather it is the fulfillment of Jesus' promise to the Samaritan woman that he would give her the Holy Spirit as "a spring of water gushing up to eternal life" (John 4:14). Contemplative writers typically stress that at this point language fails us, or must be stretched to the breaking point in order to speak of this union. Perhaps the most articulate expression of this union is not found in words, but in the life itself of a saint.

SEEING AND RECEIVING

Certain other themes resurface in the writings of the contemplative or mystical tradition. I will mention two that become dominant themes in the rest of this book.

The first is *vision*. The word contemplation is often associated with "seeing," and one way of understanding the Christian mystical tradition is that it seeks a new way of seeing. This begins with discerning the mystery of God in scripture and sacraments, but it spills over into how we see everything. It involves seeing "through" the realities of this world to its most fundamental reality, which is that God holds it in existence. But it also involves seeing "through" our illusions about ourselves and others. It involves seeing ourselves and others in light of our most fundamental reality, which is that we are loved by God.

The second is *receptivity*. The three phases of contemplative life that I outlined above can give the false impression that the Christian mystical tradition is about what we can achieve in our journey to God. Nothing could be farther from the truth. What mystical vision sees is that all that we are is a gift. The end of all our striving is to realize that it has not been we who have been striving, but rather God's Spirit has been striving within us; it is not we who have been praying, but the Spirit who prays within us, "with sighs too deep for words" (Romans 8:26). Rather than being a technique for self-salvation, the path of the mystical tradition is simply a way of recognizing one's fundamental receptivity before God and of entrusting oneself to God's Spirit.

WHY THE MYSTICS MATTER NOW

These two fundamental themes return us to the question of why the mystics matter or, more pointedly, why they matter *now*. We live in a world that, in some ways, considers itself to have outgrown religion (despite all evidence to the contrary), a world that has profound faith in science to deliver The Truth. What could this mystical tradition offer our world? Perhaps mystics mattered when religion was all people had to console them, but why should they matter *now*?

My answer to this question lies in the rest of this book. In what follows, I try to show how contemporary life presents us with certain challenges, some of which are unique to our era, others of which are as old as the human race. I also try to show how the resources of the Christian mystical tradition can help us, both Christians and non-Christians, in puzzling through those challenges. At times I may sound quite negative about our modern world, but in fact I think it no better nor worse than any other era. Of course in some people's eyes this itself will condemn me, since they are convinced that human history is progressive and that our era is better than all that came before. I freely admit that I do not believe this. Indeed, some of our world's biggest problems are at the same time its greatest achievements. The vast array of genuinely good things the modern world offers us can overwhelm and defeat us. The very progress that makes such a good life possible for some of us is also the progress that degrades our environment and leaves so many others in abject poverty.

But my point is not to vilify the modern world. It offers too many joys unique to itself (roller coasters spring to mind) to warrant such treatment. In pointing to our modern dilemmas and perplexities I am simply trying to open a space in our self-confidence so that we might hear echo the sometimes familiar, sometimes alien voices of the mystics. For unless we hear them, we will never know how much they matter.

1 | How to Live in a World Without God

Thérèse of Lisieux
and the Trial of Faith

At this time I was enjoying such a living faith, such a clear faith, *that the thought of heaven made up all my happiness, and I was unable to believe that there were really impious people who had no faith. I believed that they were actually speaking against their own inner conviction when they denied the existence of heaven, that beautiful heaven where God Himself wanted to be their Eternal Reward. During those very joyful days of the Easter season, Jesus made me feel that there were really souls who have no faith, and who, through the abuse of grace, lost this precious treasure, the source of the only real and pure joys. He permitted my soul to be invaded by the thickest darkness, and that the thought of heaven, up until then so sweet to me, be no longer anything but the cause of struggle and torment. This trial was not to last a few days or a few weeks, it was not to be extinguished until the hour set by God Himself and this hour has not yet come. . . .*

When I want to rest my heart fatigued by the darkness which surrounds it by the memory of the luminous country after which I aspire, my torment redoubles; it seems to me that the darkness, borrowing the voice of sinners, says mockingly to me: "You are dreaming about the light, about a fatherland embalmed in the sweetest perfumes; you are dreaming about the eternal possession of the creator of all

these marvels; you believe that one day you will walk out of this fog which surrounds you! Advance, advance; rejoice in death which will give you not what you hope for but a night still more profound, the night of nothingness."
—*Thérèse of Lisieux (1873–1897)*
The Story of a Soul

Frequently I hear the opinion that, on the whole, people are a lot less religious than they used to be. This is a view that is often expressed by the undergraduates I teach, who are trying to explain how alien they find the world view of, say, the prophet Jeremiah or Saint Augustine. I tell them that many of the contemporaries of Jeremiah and Augustine also found their world views quite alien and that people have never been terribly religious, but these students persist in believing that somehow things are different today. They believe that their world is stripped of God's presence in a way that makes the unbelief of today different from the unbelief spoken of by the Biblical writer: "Fools say in their hearts, 'There is no God.'"

Despite evidence of ancient unbelief, I think my students are right: there *is* something different about the unbelief of today. Certainly people of other times have felt bereft of God. But today the very question of God itself—which once seemed so pervasive as to be unavoidable—can in most cases simply be ignored. Atheism no longer takes the form of an individual's active rejection of God, a protest against the very idea of God. Rather it has become the blasé default mode of a culture that has found that it can get along quite well without God.

We might say that there is an atheism that is woven into the very fabric of contemporary life. Even those who believe in God or the Divine or a Higher Power are, for the most part, able to go through their days without much reference to that belief. As science describes more and more of the universe's mechanisms and as technology enables us more and more to manipulate those mechanisms, the place of God seems to diminish. When our child is sick we first call the pediatrician, not the priest. When we want to understand human behavior we consult the psychologist, not the prophet. In looking to the future we hope in our mutual funds, not a messiah. God is invoked, if at all, to deal with things like death, inexplicable human evil, or natural disasters—those extremities that we have not managed to explain or control . . . at least not yet. But time and technology march on and God's days seem numbered.

To put a word on this, I would say that we perceive our world as "disenchanted." The sociologist Max Weber used this term to describe how modern people have come increasingly to see their world as subject to their own rational management and decreasingly to see it as subject to the providence of God or gods. The general presumption of our Western culture, at least since the Renaissance, is that the world is something to be mastered and managed by human effort. We are not helpless before the powers that bear down upon us; rather we can take the raw material of nature and fashion for ourselves a livable world.

This confidence has brought many material benefits to us, but it has also brought problems, not least in our decimation of the environment. But this idea of humans as the masters of the world is not simply the vision of the technocrats who want to "pave paradise and put up a parking lot." It is equally the perspective of those who wish to preserve the environment. Efforts to save endangered species or to ensure biodiversity or to manage our natural resources are ironically exercises of our mastery over a nature that once mastered us. It might be a benign mastery, but it is still mastery.

Of course the human struggle to dominate nature is as old as the book of Genesis, when God tells Adam and Eve, "Be fruitful and multiply, and fill the earth and subdue it; and have dominion over the fish of the sea and over the birds of the air and over every living thing that moves upon the earth" (Genesis 1:28). But there is a difference, for the author of Genesis clearly portrays the human beings as acting at God's behest, as God's appointed agents. The dominion they exercise over the earth is simply an extension of the dominion God exercises as the world's creator. Their labor is a task imbued with divine significance and they will ultimately be held accountable for how well or ill they have carried out that task.

Things are different now. Our control over the world no longer serves the purposes of God but rather *our* purposes. We do not simply tend the world as if it were a garden owned by another, but we have come to take possession of the garden itself. As such, the world has no meaning that is given with it, no significance beyond what we assign to it, no plan to be carried out. The things that we encounter—the rocks and plants and animals—no longer come to us as a cosmos endowed with a divine purpose, but simply as inert matter that *we* must form, as a random collection of objects that *we* endow with meaning. Our sense of having a duty to make the world meaningful, as Weber put it, "prowls about in our lives like the ghost of dead religious beliefs."

A DISENCHANTED WORLD

The German theologian and martyr Dietrich Bonhoeffer, in letters written while imprisoned by the Nazis, spoke of this disenchanted modern world as one that had "come of age," a world that has increasingly less need for God to fill the gaps in our knowledge and power. The great mistake for Christians, according to Bonhoeffer, was to try and convince this world-come-of-age that it was still a child, that in some secret, hidden way it was still religious.

Bonhoeffer was arguing against the view of various Christians in the nineteenth and twentieth centuries who, in responding to the disenchantment of the world, argued that while on the surface our lives are disenchanted, on a deeper level we retain a deep longing for the divine. Indeed, those who argued in this way felt that if human beings were to fully engage their being at its very core then they would be confronted with the fact that they already had an unarticulated awareness of God, a drive to transcend the merely worldly. So, according to this view, there is a sense in which everyone, deep down, *is* religious. They simply do not realize it. And for many people it takes a radical confrontation with illness or death or evil before this subterranean belief surfaces.

Bonhoeffer, in contrast, felt that we must take people at their word when they say that they don't believe in God, or that the existence or nonexistence of God is of no concern to them. Indeed, the very arrangement of modern life, with its very pragmatic orientation towards "getting the job done," and its impatience with abstract questions about truth or goodness or beauty, indicates that people *can* get along without God, precisely because what counts today as "getting along" excludes such exotica as religion.

The attempt to make everyone covertly religious implied that those who were unaware of their covert religiosity were simply not seriously engaging with the important questions of life. Bonhoeffer's response to this was that we should not accuse those without belief of a lack of seriousness. Many of them are engaged with extremely serious endeavors, such as running nations or making scientific discoveries or raising children. We should not assume that the *important* questions of life are those that concern death and sickness, but rather those that concern life and health. If God is truly God, then God must be found in the center of everyday life, not in its margins; in health, not just in sickness; in life, not just in death. But for many it is precisely their everyday lives that have become disenchanted; it is in everyday life that human mastery most exerts itself.

We might say that part of what is distinctive about modern unbelief is that the *coup d'etat* by which we have usurped God's place has become for many the normal mode of existence. At the same time, there are some who do feel the loss of God, who feel it acutely. I count myself among those who find the task of filling the world's abyss of meaning to be an overwhelming one, who find it difficult enough to manage my own life without assistance, much less manage the world. How can someone who forgets to pay the mortgage endow the world with meaning? So I find myself wanting to occupy a world that is transparent to *divine* meaning. But I also recognize that I cannot make it so simply by an act of my own will.

If those who feel no need for God should not be accused of a lack of seriousness, then those who yearn to see God's face should not be accused of nostalgia. I fully acknowledge that when my child is sick I think of the pediatrician first and prayer second, if at all. I will not pretend that I can live in the sacred cosmos of Jeremiah or Augustine (though they too had difficulty discerning God at times). If I affirm with Jeremiah that it is God "who made the earth by his power, who established the world by his wisdom, and by his understanding stretched out the heavens" (Jeremiah 10:12), I cannot pretend that the earth or the heavens declare this unambiguously to my modern mind, shaped as it is by the pronouncements of modern science. And if I say with Augustine, "God, you have made us for yourself, and our hearts are restless until they rest in you," I cannot help but add to myself, "or perhaps until we take our Prozac."

I too live in this world in which it has become very easy to ignore the question of God, to slip into a blasé disbelief. Like Bonhoeffer, I am unwilling to say that if I simply look deeply enough into myself I will discover an experience of God. I am too aware of those voices that tell me that if I look deep within I will find only strands of DNA that are the product of random mutation and natural selection. I don't want to put myself in the position of telling people that they really, deep, deep down, have an experience of God that they either do not recognize or will not acknowledge.

So, like many of my neighbors, I live in a world grown opaque to divine meaning and purpose. My everyday experience speaks little of God's presence. But it is easy to appeal to one's experience; it is much harder to make sense of it or to know its significance. The experience of God's absence *may* indicate God's unreality and the disenchantment of the world. But it may also indicate that the world awaits enchantment and that the everyday is precisely the point of God's arrival. As Walter Benjamin put it, "every second of time . . . [is] the straight gate through which the Messiah might enter."

THE WORLD AS A MYSTIC SEES IT

It is perhaps natural to assume that being a "mystic" involves an experience of the divine that is so immediate, of such clarity and certainty, that one cannot doubt it. Mystics seem to have an experience— whether visions or voices or trances or a profound sense of unity with the divine—that in some sense inoculates them against unbelief. If this were the case, then they wouldn't have much to say to those of us who have not shared their particular experience, and especially not to those who experience God's absence, who are beset with doubts about God or the divine or the meaningfulness of any and every thing. For those who look at the world and see a mechanism without an operator, it seems that the mystics *can't* matter, because we do not share their fundamental assumption that God is something or someone that can be directly and indubitably experienced.

But what if we are wrong in thinking this? What if the experience of the mystic is not always one of light and certainty, but rather sometimes one of darkness and doubt? What if the mystic too sees a world opaque to divine meaning and purpose?

In the Fall of 1897 a twenty-four year old Carmelite nun named Thérèse Martin lay in a French monastery, dying of tuberculosis. Thérèse, who after her death would come to be known as the "Little Flower," seems an unlikely person to turn to for tough-minded talk about the modern experience of disenchantment. Raised in an extremely devout Catholic family, she was surrounded by the rejection of the modern world and the sticky-sweet piety that were both so typical of nineteenth-century French Catholicism. Early on in life she seems to have experienced something of the ecstasies and illuminations that many associate with mysticism. But in the memoir that she wrote in the final years of her life she records an experience of constant spiritual darkness—what has come to be called her "trial of faith"—with an unblinking honesty that can startle even the most skeptical unbeliever. God does not come to comfort her in her dying distress; she *feels* the absence of God at the very extremity at which many would hope for God to appear.

Like some other Christians in the nineteenth century, Thérèse at first found it difficult to accept that anyone could disbelieve in God. In her particular case, the strong piety of her home had protected her as much as possible from the corrosive skepticism of the modern world. She had felt in the very depths of her heart that heaven was her true homeland: "*I was enjoying such a living faith, such a clear faith, that the thought of heaven made up all my happiness.*" Indeed, for her the heavenly country seemed more real than the earthly. Writing of her feelings upon contemplating heaven she said, "I seem to be receiving the embraces of Jesus. I believe I see my heavenly Mother coming to meet me with Papa, Mama, the four little angels. I believe I am enjoying forever a real and eternal family reunion."

This strong experience of the reality of heaven led Thérèse to feel that unbelievers "*were actually speaking against their own inner conviction when they denied the existence of heaven.*" If the impious were honest with themselves, they would have to acknowledge that their unbelief was simply a matter of their own hard-heartedness or lack of seriousness. The experience of Godlessness was, in her view, simply not a possibility.

But this changes for Thérèse when, as she puts it, her soul is "*invaded by the thickest darkness.*" Thérèse speaks but little of this experience, because she did not want to tempt her fellow nuns to disbelief, but it is clear that this darkness so clouded her sense of heaven as her true homeland that *"the thought of heaven, up until then so sweet to me,"* became nothing *"but the cause of struggle and torment."* A belief that once came easily and naturally to her seems to have become impossible, incredible. She comes to see that it is in fact possible that one's *"inner conviction"* might speak *against* the reality of God.

NOT CLARITY, BUT DARKNESS

In short, what Thérèse experiences is not clarity, but darkness, not the presence of God, but God's absence. In the Christian mystical tradition such periods of darkness or "spiritual dryness" are hardly unknown. Indeed they are seen as part and parcel of anyone's spiritual journey. Christian mystics speak of experiencing both "consolations" (strong feelings of God's love and presence) and "desolations" (strong feelings of God's absence), and generally advise that too much store not be put in either of them.

But one of the distinctive things about Thérèse's experience is that her desolation does not pass: *"This trial was not to last a few days or a few weeks, it was not to be extinguished until the hour set by God Himself and this hour has not yet come."* The darkness is not simply part of the rhythm of her spiritual life; it becomes her spiritual life *in its entirety.* As she describes it, her desolation is unrelieved; she is constantly plagued by doubts. So if she is to continue to love God, then she must find a way of doing so that can dwell within the experience of God's absence.

Thérèse's experience of darkness is a matter of personal crisis, but she also connects it quite explicitly to the experience of the disenchantment of the world. In a conversation with her sister Pauline shortly before her death, Thérèse said, "If you only knew what frightful thoughts obsess me! . . . It's the reasoning of the worst materialists which is imposed upon my mind: Later, unceasingly making new advances, science will explain everything naturally. . . ." The doubts that plague her are so typical of our world: what if we explain everything so completely that there is no room left for God? Such thoughts seem to mock her earlier beliefs, showing them to be childish fantasies.

The darkness that surrounds her even mocks the hope that death might deliver her from her doubts: "*Advance, advance; rejoice in death which will give you not what you hope for but a night still more profound, the night of nothingness.*" Death is not a passage into the heavenly homeland, but annihilation. She can take no refuge in the hope that God will appear at the extremity of death; all that the darkness of her experience promises is the most profound darkness of all: the night of nothingness.

And death was a very present reality for Thérèse. A year after her "trial of faith" began, Thérèse fell gravely ill with tuberculosis. She was to live only five more months, slowly dying by a suffocation that seemed almost the physical embodiment of the spiritual suffocation that she was already undergoing. Pointing out the window to a shadow on the landscape, she said to one of the sisters attending her sickbed, "Look! Do you see the black hole where we can see nothing; it's in a similar hole that I am as far as body and soul are concerned. Ah! what darkness! But I am at peace."

AT PEACE WITH GOD'S ABSENCE

Peace? Are these simply the pious mouthings of one too afraid to admit the depths of her despair, a kind of spiritual whistling past the graveyard? How does one find peace in the black hole of disenchantment? How can one love God as she lies suffocating, dying bit by bit both physically and spiritually? But this is the challenge Thérèse takes up: to find God in the daily experience of God's absence and of physical pain.

Perhaps the genius of Thérèse's spirituality is that she locates the encounter with God in the midst of what, in the modern-day world, seems most bereft of God: everyday life. She described herself as following a "little way"—a spiritual path made up not of great sacrifices or extraordinary experiences, but of trying to bring the love of the crucified Jesus to the most mundane, seemingly Godless, situations. Whether this was a matter of being splashed with dirty dishwater or of being seated in chapel near a nun who constantly made irritating noises, Thérèse saw everyday life as constantly presenting us with opportunities to respond with love rather than anger, irritation, or disgust. And when Thérèse entered into the darkness of her trial of faith, when God fled from her experience, she persisted in seeking God in the everyday. Faithfulness to the God she could no longer see took the form of love and generosity toward her fellow nuns, whom she could see. Heaven may have been closed to her, prayer may have become painful, but by her taking up the task of bringing Jesus' love into each moment of her day, Thérèse sought to re-enchant those moments, even if this re-enchantment was a reality that remained hidden from her.

TRUSTING THE ABYSS

God was to be sought in the everyday, and in the final months of her life the everyday reality of Thérèse was agony of both body and soul. Thérèse sought to understand both her physical and spiritual sufferings as a mysterious purification of her faith and an initiation into a deeper understanding of God's love. The danger of spiritual consolation is that we come to depend on the consolation to undergird our faith, to love the experience of consolation rather than God. God becomes the Prince Charming of an enchanted fairy tale, lavishing gifts upon his beloved. But such faith and love are fragile things, subject to disenchantment. Thérèse's trial of faith requires her to abandon this fragile faith and cling with desperate stubbornness to the Jesus who cried out on the cross, "My God, my God, why have you abandoned me?"

It is precisely when God is most hidden from Thérèse, when she is gripped by the Godlessness of her experience, that she turns her faith entirely over to God and her love for God is fused with God's infinite love for her. Viewed through the stubborn eyes of naked faith, her experience of God's absence is transformed into the experience of a God who far surpasses the fairy tale God—a God whose love for her is so immense that from her limited human perspective it feels indistinguishable from *"the night of nothingness."* She writes: "Your love has gone before me, and it has grown with me, and now it is an abyss whose depths I cannot fathom." Thérèse must trust the abyss, must greet it as the infinity of God's love and not as God's annihilating absence. But she must do this *against* all evidence, *against* all feeling. She must abandon herself to the love of a God whom she cannot see or feel: "Now, abandonment alone guides me. I have no other compass."

One way in which Thérèse's trial of faith is different from much modern unbelief is that she does not resign herself to blasé atheism. Rather, she actively seizes upon the Godlessness of the world and of her experience and understands it as a path to God, or rather God's path to her. For Thérèse, the experience of God's absence becomes what Jesus meant by "poverty of spirit." It is to the poor, the hungry, and the mourning that Jesus promises the kingdom. The soul deprived of God is paradoxically filled with God because, in her desire for the God who eludes her, she is transformed into love itself. In a letter to one of her sisters she wrote, "Ah! let us remain then *very far* from all that sparkles, let us love our littleness, let us love to feel nothing, then we shall be poor in spirit, and Jesus will come to look for us, and *however far* we may be, He will transform us in flames of love."

WHY THÉRÈSE MATTERS NOW

Peace. Not the peace of blasé resignation. As Thérèse lay dying she spoke to her fellow nuns who surrounded her bed: "Little sisters! . . . Little sisters! . . .

My God! . . . My God, have pity on me! I can't take
anymore! . . . I can't take anymore! . . . And yet I must
endure. . . . I am . . . I am reduced . . . No, I would never
have believed one could suffer so much. . . never!
never! . . . ." And looking at the crucifix, she said, "Oh!
I love Him. . . . My God, I love You! . . ."

This is the voice of one in the midst of flames, being
consumed, reduced. It is the voice of one for whom all
guiding stars are clouded over, who must now entrust
herself to the immensity of the sea. It is the voice of one
for whom every second of time has become the straight
gate through which the Messiah might enter. It is the
voice of one who, in the midst of a disenchanted world,
re-enchants it by surrendering all—all plans, all control,
all love—to the God who eludes her experience.

2 | How to Live in a World with Too Many Gods

Ignatius of Loyola
on the Discernment of Spirits

Human beings are created to praise, reverence, and serve God our Lord, and by means of this to save their souls.

The other things on the face of the earth are created for human beings, to help them in working toward the end for which they are created.

From this it follows that I should use these things to the extent that they help me toward my end, and rid myself of them to the extent that they hinder me.

To do this, I must make myself indifferent to all created things, in regard to everything which is left to my freedom of will and is not forbidden. Consequently, on my own part I ought not to seek health rather than sickness, wealth rather than poverty, honor rather than dishonor, a long life rather than a short one, and so on in all other matters.

I ought to desire and elect only the thing which is more conducive to the end for which I am created.

—*Ignatius Loyola (1491–1556)*
"Principle and Foundation" of the Spiritual Exercises

The disenchanted world that we live in is paradoxically also a world of amazing credulity. It sometimes seems that we will believe almost anything. There are obvious examples: shops that trade in crystals and aromatherapies, psychic hotlines, bizarre cults that await space aliens who will take them to the promised land. But the credulity of our world runs deeper than these easily dismissible cases. There is a profound willingness among us to give unquestioned adherence to a whole host of authoritative voices.

For example, many of the same students who sit in my classes convinced that people of today can no longer believe in the way that their ancestors did have at the same time a belief in science that I can best characterize as superstitious. They have an unshakable faith that science delivers Truth to them, but most do not have even a passing knowledge of contemporary scientific debates. And when presented with an account of these debates, many of them cower more abjectly than any so-called primitive people worshiping their local idol: "This is *science*; we can't possibly understand *this*." Indeed, part of the attraction of modern science to their minds is that it is seems so hopelessly complicated that they cannot possibly be expected to actually understand it; they must simply submit.

One might add other examples, such as the way in which we profess deep cynicism about government, yet entrust so much of our lives to the very bureaucrats that we claim to distrust and despise, or the way in which we decry modern materialism, yet sacrifice our dreams for the sake of financial security. But suffice it to say that the disenchantment of the world has not proved to be the demise of the gods. In fact, as the world grows opaque to any *single* divine meaning and purpose, we often find ourselves confronted with a plurality of meanings and purposes that exert claims on us. We are beset not by one god, but by many: the state, the market, the family, our various peer groups. One might say that our Godlessness has returned us to a situation of polytheism.

In his book *Joyful Wisdom*, Friedrich Nietzsche tells of a "madman" who runs into the marketplace announcing the death of God. The madman asks, "Who gave us the sponge to wipe away the whole horizon? What did we do when we loosened this earth from its sun?" In these words the madman expresses the sense that, with the passing of God, life has lost any overall sense of direction or purpose. Like the horizon, God loomed at the edge of our awareness as a point by which we oriented ourselves. Now we have no such point. The world has lost its center. We are like planets without a sun to define their orbit; we go spinning off in a variety of directions.

So we live in what is sometimes described as a situation of radical pluralism. We are confronted with a variety of voices, all contending for our attention, and we seem to have no fixed place in which to stand in choosing among them. In society we seek to solve this problem by dividing our lives into their private aspects, where we may listen to whatever authorities we choose, and their public aspects, where we obey a minimal set of laws that are designed to help us to simply get along with each other but not to lead us to any common goal. Individuals and groups are free to pursue their own directions and purposes so long as they don't interfere with other people pursuing *their* own directions and purposes. This is what we today call a pluralistic society and it bears more than a passing resemblance to the polytheism of the Roman Empire. The Romans were quite happy to let people worship their own gods, so long as they gave a minimal respect to the gods who protected the city of Rome. And, at least in many people's estimations, it worked quite well in ancient Rome and has worked quite well in modern America.

However, the public and private spheres of our lives cannot be quite so neatly segregated and the pluralism that characterizes our society also characterizes us as individuals. It is not simply that we no longer have a shared, societal horizon that we all look to. In many cases our personal horizons have been wiped clean as well and we find ourselves unable to orient ourselves so as to find a direction to pursue. Many different voices call to us—family, career, self-fulfillment, material goods—and we seem to lack an overarching framework within which to locate them so that we can listen to and make judgments about their claims upon us. All of these things seem good, all of their voices are beautiful, and we want to respond to them all. In our private as well as our public lives we find ourselves drawn to the worship of many gods.

CHOOSING BETWEEN GOOD AND BETTER

It is a tempting simplicity to think that the wiping away of the horizon that Nietzsche's madman describes is primarily a "moral" problem; that, with the eclipse of God, people have lost any ability to distinguish between good and evil. And certainly we hear of people who seem to lack any moral compass, who commit atrocities in the name of the reigning ideology, who obey whatever orders their leaders might give them. But this is hardly a new phenomenon, nor is it one particularly associated with godlessness. In 1099 A.D. European crusaders pillaged the City of Jerusalem, brutally murdering its inhabitants in the name of the Prince of Peace.

Likewise, most of us are able to avoid committing ourselves to obviously silly pursuits. It is not too difficult to avoid calling psychic hotlines (at least more than once) or giving all our money to some shady character in a long beard and a white robe. For most of us, these things might pique a passing interest, but they are not besetting temptations.

No, the real difficulty is that we confront choices not between good and evil, or the serious and the trivial, but between good and better. Most of us have some sense of what is evil (even if we sometimes cannot explain *why* we think something is evil) and, on a day-to-day basis, we usually manage to do the good. We don't live in fear that we will empty our bank accounts into the pocket of some charlatan or embark on a spiritual snipe hunt. But how do we choose between those many things that are genuinely, undeniably, good?

To take one example, many people today, particularly women but not just women, find themselves torn between the demands of work and of family. For some this dilemma is one imposed by economic necessity (they need to work in order to support their families) but in many cases people work because they want to, not because they have to. And even in those cases where people work because they have to, they find that working is something they value beyond the money it provides. Yet it seems that too often they feel that both their careers and their families suffer because of compromises that must be made, time that must be parceled out, attention that is constantly shifting. For many, this division in their lives is a source of tension and unhappiness. And even in cases of people who do only one of these things, work or family, they constantly feel the pull to do the other as well. Shouldn't I be working outside the home? Isn't it time to start a family?

The source of unhappiness in such cases is not that we want something bad for us, but that we are torn between two things that are genuinely *good*. It is *good* to have a family, to be available to spouse and children, to create and maintain a home. But likewise, it is *good* to work at a job, to hone and exercise your skills in your chosen field, to produce something and to be rewarded for it. Pulled between these two goods, we find our hearts divided and unhappy.

Søren Kierkegaard said, "purity of heart is to will one thing." By this definition, our heart becomes "impure" not when it wills something evil (how often do we actually will something evil?) but when it wills conflicting goods. The word "purity" conjures images of something uncontaminated—as when we speak of pure water or air. Our hearts are impure because every intention we form, every resolution we make, every goal we set, is constantly being invaded by other intentions, resolutions, or goals. We have too many choices, too many options, too many goods from which to choose. Our hearts become unfocused as we flit from attraction to attraction, never entering fully into one thing before we feel pulled in a different direction by some other thing.

FOCUSED SINGLE-MINDEDNESS

So then, is it simply a matter of choosing? Of gritting our teeth and rejecting one good in favor of another? Of forcing ourselves to be more single minded? Maybe. But doesn't this sound like a diminished form of life? We can easily imagine someone who wills one thing and one thing only, say a woman who "lives for her children" or a man who "lives for his job." But this isn't the sort of life most of us aspire to, and rightly so. The children grow up and leave home. We retire. Those who live for their children or their jobs often find themselves later in life feeling bitter that they have invested so much in one thing. It does not seem right to live life less fully simply in order to maintain purity of heart.

It is ironic that the more fully we seek to live our lives the harder it is to keep our hearts focused. An admirable openness makes us listen to the many voices that call to us. A commendable enthusiasm for living leads us to scatter our time and energy among a host of pursuits. Yet such a scattered existence can be profoundly draining, precisely because we have no way of coordinating the things to which we give ourselves. We seek to worship many gods, but seem to be able to give none of them their due.

How can we achieve purity of heart—focused single mindedness—while still acknowledging and appreciating the variety of goods that call to us? How can we give ourselves to people and pursuits without losing ourselves to them? Where, amid the babble of voices, do we find the one voice that, if we follow it, can integrate all our dreams, desires, and activities into a coherent, livable life?

WHAT GIVES US JOY

Such questions are not simply our questions; they were also the questions of a sixteenth-century Basque knight named Iñigo, who came to be known as Ignatius of Loyola. Ignatius was a man of powerful imagination and passion. He loved to envision the dashing figure he would make at court, the battles he would win, the ladies he would charm. After having his leg shattered in battle by a cannonball, Ignatius spent a long period of time convalescing. During this time, in order to make the days pass, he asked for some books to read. Before being wounded he had been very fond of chivalric romances, which had sparked his imagination and filled his head with visions of himself as the ideal knight. But the house where he was staying didn't have any of these books and instead he was given a story of the life of Christ and a book of the lives of the saints.

Deprived of any other reading material, Ignatius began to read these books, approaching them in much the same way he had approached the romances. Between the times spent reading, he would let his imagination wander, absorbed in thought sometimes for two or three hours. He wrote in his autobiography that he would often imagine "what he would do in the service of a certain lady; the means he would take so he could go to the place where she lived; the quips—the words he would address to her; the feats of arms he would perform in her service." However, at other times his imagination would take him in a different direction, and he would ask "What if I should do what St. Francis did, and what St. Dominic did?" And so for a while he let his imagination fantasize about exploits both sacred and secular.

He began to notice a difference between those times when he imagined himself engaged in some knightly pursuit and those times when he imagined himself doing the kinds of things done by St. Francis and St. Dominic. He enjoyed imagining his exploits as a knight but afterwards he found that he felt "dry and dissatisfied." But when he imagined himself going on pilgrimage to Jerusalem or doing some other act of religious devotion, he enjoyed it no less than his knightly fantasies, and afterwards, rather than feeling dissatisfied, he felt "satisfied and joyful." This recognition that some thoughts left him sad and other thoughts left him joyful became the key to what he would call "the discernment of spirits."

Upon recovering, Ignatius traveled to Montserrat, near Barcelona, where he left his knight's sword at the altar of the Virgin Mary and exchanged clothes with a beggar. These actions were symbolic of his newfound resolve to live solely for the honor and glory of God. But his spiritual journey was just beginning. He spent the next year in the town of Manresa, living off alms and spending much of the day in prayer. During this time he had a number of extraordinary experiences, including visions of the Trinity, of the humanity of Christ, and a recurring vision of an incredibly beautiful object whose details he could not make out. He also suffered from the spiritual disease known as "scrupulosity," which is an inability to believe that one's sins have been forgiven, even though they have been confessed and absolved. The word "scruples" comes from the Latin word *scrupulus*, which refers to a small sharp stone. Like a stone in his shoe, Ignatius' past sins nagged at him, inhibiting his progress on his spiritual journey.

Given these various experiences, it is perhaps not surprising that much of Ignatius' time at Manresa was spent trying to figure out how one distinguishes between genuine spiritual experiences, and delusional or false ones. Should he pay attention to his sense of continuing sinfulness? Was there perhaps some sin he had forgotten to confess? Should he accept all his visions as genuine, or might some of them be deceptive and destructive? How could one possibly judge?

After much time Ignatius began to notice that some things, such as his visions of the Trinity and the humanity of Christ, filled him with an enduring sense of peace and joy—what the Christian tradition calls "consolation"—while others, such as his worries about his past sins, not only were joyless, but seemed to be in direct conflict with his experience of consolation. Other experiences, however, called for more subtle discernment. Ignatius came to see that while his enjoyment of the beautiful but indistinct object increased each time he beheld it, so too did the bitterness and disappointment he felt when the vision ended. Much like his imaginings of his knightly exploits, this vision provided passing enjoyment, but not enduring consolation. Indeed, its long-term effect was a joylessness that more closely resembled the effect of his scruples than the effect of his other visions. Such a vision, Ignatius decided, could not be from God or to God's glory.

A Way of Seeing

Ignatius' experiences at Manresa formed the basis for what would become his *Spiritual Exercises*, which are a kind of manual for those who, like Ignatius, seek to live their lives entirely for the greater glory of God and who, again like Ignatius, wish to help others do the same. Ignatius would go on to do many things—most famously to found the Society of Jesus, commonly called the Jesuits—but behind them all were certain key lessons he learned in his year at Manresa. It was there that he began to learn how one could judge between different possible courses of action.

He had come to realize during his convalescence that only in God could his various hopes and desires be reconciled, and he had learned how to distinguish the good from the evil and the trivial, but the question remained: What exactly was he supposed to *do*? His original plan was to go to Jerusalem to live permanently among the holy sites. This, no doubt, was a good thing to do. However, circumstances forced him to return to Europe, where he decided that he should further his education "so he would be able to help souls." This too was, no doubt, a good thing. But which was the better thing? If living in Jerusalem was better, must he live his life in permanent regret that he could not do so? Later, when Ignatius and six friends took vows of poverty and service to others, thus forming the nucleus of the Jesuits, he again was faced with this question, now not only for himself, but for his companions as well. What should they *do*? Many things needed doing in sixteenth-century Europe. How to pick among all the possible worthy tasks?

What he learned in his time at Manresa was not so much a specific path he was to take as it was a method for seeing, at any given moment, which path before him was *ad maiorum Dei gloriam* ("to the greater glory of God"—the motto of the Jesuits). He came to see that the discernment of spirits requires time, patience, and constant attention. When considering a possible path to be followed, one should notice whether the consideration of it produces an enduring sense of joy and a long-term increase in faith, hope, and love, or whether its pleasures are only passing. One must not choose hastily, because the immediately attractive thing is not always the best. A path that is initially unattractive might, upon further experience and reflection, prove to be better than that path to which we were first drawn. Thus, in the case of Ignatius, his initial attraction to chivalric romances did not prove as enduring as the attraction exerted by the initially unappealing stories of Christ and the saints. More profoundly, when his initial plan to live the rest of his life in Jerusalem was thwarted, he concluded that this was not the path God intended for him. To have dwelt on his disappointment would have mired him in a bitterness that is incompatible with the profound joy of true consolation. Rather than cling to thwarted plans, one must patiently wait to see which new path God opens up.

THE ONE PATH

At the head of the *Spiritual Exercises* stands what is known as the Principle and Foundation. Here Ignatius articulates how single-mindedness of purpose not only does not conflict with a diversity of goods, but actually supports that diversity. Let me explain what this means.

Ignatius begins by claiming that human beings have one overarching purpose to their existence: *"to praise, reverence, and serve God our Lord, and by means of this to save their souls."* This is simply another way of saying what St. Augustine prayed: "you have made us for yourself, and our heart is restless until it rests in you." As creatures who have come forth from God, our proper destiny is to return to God, and we make this return by loving God through praise, reverence, and service.

For Ignatius, as for Augustine, this purpose is not a matter of choice; we do not have the option of living for

God or living for something else. Since God is nothing less than the source of everything that is, it is not as if the path to God is one path among others; it is the only path. To leave this path is to wander restlessly through thickets of nothingness until we fall victim to the nonbeing of death. Unlike those who would posit an irreducible diversity of goals, a multiplicity of private and public gods, Ignatius presents us with a vision in which everyone and everything shares the same ultimate source and goal. As Ignatius sees it, to believe that there is but one God is to seek a comprehensive good that all beings share, which makes it impossible to see our individual goals as our own private affairs.

Where we might properly speak about "choice" (or what Ignatius calls "electing") is in the variety of ways in which we might *praise, reverence, and serve God.* For Ignatius believes that everything that exists is a gift from God to human beings, *to help them in working toward the end for which they are created.* Note that Ignatius believes that *everything* can, at least in principle, be of use to us in praising, reverencing, and serving God. Nothing is excluded out of hand, because everything has God as its source.

Thus, I cannot simply decide from the start that helping the poor is "just not my thing" because "my thing" is becoming as rich and comfortable as I possibly can, regardless of how it affects my relationship with God or others. Neither can I decide that *only* living off alms in Jerusalem will fulfill me, because living in Jerusalem, while perhaps a good thing, is ultimately only a means to the more encompassing—the all-encompassing—good of resting in God. Ignatius pushes us to see how the things that we choose fit into a larger, shared conception of our source and purpose.

Therefore, I ought to *"use these things to the extent that they help me toward my end, and rid myself of them to the extent that they hinder me."* The relevant question to ask about anything is whether it enables me to better *praise, reverence, and serve God.* Does acquiring massive amounts of wealth do this? Does helping the poor? Does living off alms in Jerusalem?

Rather than immediately answering such questions, Ignatius exhorts us to be *indifferent to all created things.* By "indifferent" Ignatius does not mean uncaring. What he means is that we must see that the differences between our various options are radically relativized by our common purpose. *All* things can, at least potentially, be done—or given up—for God. As a result, Ignatius says, *"I ought not to seek health rather than sickness, wealth rather than poverty, honor rather than dishonor, a long life rather than a short one."* Here he echoes Paul: "I have learned to be content with whatever I have. I know what it is to have little, and I know what it is to have plenty. In any and all circumstances I have learned the secret of being well-fed and of going hungry, of having plenty and of being in need. I can do all things through him who strengthens me" (Philippians 4:11–13).

Ignatius and Paul find that belief in a single, overarching purpose to all things does not restrict our freedom or stifle diversity, rather it frees us to choose things that previously would have been unimaginable for us. What really restricts us is the tenacity with which we insist on choosing our own individual goals and relying on ourselves to realize them. Ignatius and Paul place their faith in a Goodness so comprehensive that it can embrace the diversity of goals that we pursue, while endowing them with a value and purpose beyond themselves.

CHOOSING

However, Ignatius does not leave us with "indifference." At some point we do choose this or that particular path, and our choosing is of crucial importance. Ignatius believes deeply that God wills something for us, and if we do not bring ourselves to will that thing, then we condemn ourselves to a frustrating and frustrated existence. So how do we move from indifference to willing the one thing necessary?

Let us return to Nietzsche's image of the horizon wiped away by the death of God. With his understanding of God as a goodness that can incorporate and preserve all lesser goods within itself, Ignatius might be thought of as restoring a horizon to us, allowing us to keep our balance through a "holy indifference." But an empty horizon is only of so much use. If you are lost in the desert, the horizon might help you not to tip over, but if there is nothing visible on that horizon, then you don't know how to move forward. You need a point on the horizon that you can move toward.

For Ignatius, that point is the life of Jesus of Nazareth. Jesus' human will was put entirely at the disposal of God's will. In becoming acquainted with the pattern of Jesus' life, we glimpse a point on the horizon by which we orient ourselves toward God's will for us. This is not, however, simply a matter of asking "what would Jesus do?," not least because we are confronted with situations that Jesus did not confront. Jesus was not a Basque knight. Jesus was not a working mother. Reading the Gospels will often not provide a direct answer to our questions. But Ignatius presumes that Jesus is not simply an historical figure, but a living presence whom we can encounter. This is why Ignatius does not so much seek to know *about* Jesus—what he said and did—but rather to come to know Jesus *himself*.

At the heart of Ignatius' *Spiritual Exercises* is a series of "contemplations," in which the person doing the *Exercises* imagines a scene from the life of Jesus and imaginatively enters into it. The contemplation is preceded by a request for what it is that one desires and followed by what Ignatius calls a "colloquy," in which one speaks with Christ "in the way one friend speaks to another, or a servant to one in authority." This combination of contemplation and colloquy is designed to bring the one doing the *Exercises* into a vibrant and intimate relationship with Jesus so that he becomes the ultimate standard by which one chooses a path. In his initial description of the colloquy Ignatius says, "reflect on yourself and ask: What have I done for Christ? What am I doing for Christ? What ought I to do for Christ?"

In our indifference we mirror the "indifference" of God toward creation: God loves *all* things without distinction, because all things share in God's own goodness. However, in choosing between the good things that God has made, we mirror Jesus, who lived entirely from and for the specific mission set for him by God: "My food is to do the will of him who sent me" (John 4:34). At some point we do choose, we *must* choose. And our model and guide for such choice—as Ignatius puts it, our "standard bearer"—is Jesus.

Two further features of the *Exercises* need to be pointed out. First, they have what we might call "spiritual companionship" as a necessary component. From his own experience, Ignatius knew that in asking "What have I done for Christ? What am I doing for Christ? What ought I to do for Christ?" we might not always answer the questions honestly. We need someone to accompany us in our search for the greater good. Thus everyone who undertakes the *Spiritual Exercises* is to have a "director" with whom they meet, normally on a daily basis. The director is there to help the one making the *Exercises* in various ways, but minimally he or she guards against self-serving or self-satisfied answers to these questions. For Ignatius, the discerning of God's will is simultaneously an intensely personal and an intensely *inter*-personal activity. The director cannot presume to know God's will for us, but he or she can help us not to mistake God's will for our own or to mistake the superficially pleasurable for the truly satisfying. Put simply, the director is there to help us keep our eyes on Jesus.

The other important feature of the *Exercises* is that they are usually done as a thirty-day silent retreat. Though Ignatius noted that the *Exercises* could be adapted for those unable to devote thirty consecutive days to them, his own experience of a lengthy convalescence recovering from his battle wounds shaped his understanding of the time needed to discern God's will. It was only when he let his various dreams and goals dwell in his mind for a lengthy period of time that he could distinguish between those that left him dry and dissatisfied and those that left him joyful and at peace. Confronted by the bewildering array of possible paths, it takes time to discover which will lead us to that Good that encompasses all other goodness.

Why Ignatius Matters Now

Because we put our faith in our jobs and families and money and sex to provide meaning for our lives we turn them into little gods, and, like the gods of ancient mythologies, they seem always to be in conflict with each other. In a world in which the horizon seems to have been wiped clean, we cluster around shrines to these tiny idols to find a little hope and meaning in life. What Ignatius bids us do is to lift our eyes once again to see the horizon, so that we can look beyond our conflicting and conflicted lives to see the eternal life that reconciles all conflicts. And he also bids us to turn our eyes to Jesus, as one who shares our humanity, yet in whom that infinite horizon is concentrated into a single point.

Part of Ignatius's genius was to realize that there are many things that one can do *ad maiorum Dei gloriam.*

This diversity can be seen in the order that he founded. There are Jesuits who are educators, missionaries, scientists, doctors, lawyers, artists, poets, and even one who runs a circus. These radically different activities are coordinated under a comprehensive single-mindedness. For Ignatius, the path to purity of heart is not first and foremost a path of exclusion. This is because the "one thing" that we must will is God in Christ, who is the universal source of all that is and who, in the words of the Jesuit poet Gerard Manley Hopkins, "plays in ten thousand places."

3 | How to Receive

Meister Eckhart
on Detachment

*This true possession of God depends on the disposition,
and on an inward directing of the reason and intention
toward God, not on a constant contemplation in an unchanging manner, for it would be impossible to nature to preserve
such an intention, and very laborious, and not the best thing
either. A man ought not to have a God who is just the product of his thought, nor should he be satisfied with that,
because if the thought vanished, God too would vanish. But
one ought to have a God who is present, a God who is far
above the notions of men and of all created things. That God
does not vanish, if a man does not willfully turn away from
him.*

*The man who has God essentially present to him grasps
God divinely, and to him God shines in all things; for everything tastes to him of God, and God forms himself for the
man out of all things. . . . A man cannot learn this by running away, by shunning things and shutting himself up in
an external solitude; but he must practice a solitude of the
spirit, wherever and with whomever he is. He must learn to
break through things and to grasp his God in them and form
him in himself powerfully in an essential manner. . . .*

*So a man must be penetrated with the divine presence,
and be shaped through and through with the shape of the God
he loves, and be present in him, so that God's presence may*

shine out to him without any effort. What is more, in all things let him acquire nakedness, and let him always remain free of things. But at the beginning there must be attentiveness and a careful formation within himself, like a schoolboy setting himself to learn.

—Meister Eckhart (c. 1260–1327)
Counsels on Discernment §7

In his book *The Future of an Illusion,* Sigmund Freud proposes the idea that our concept of God is an illusion constructed out of bits of our personal and communal histories. More precisely, we project onto the impersonal forces of nature the character of a father in order to make our helplessness before those forces more tolerable. Religion is the obsessional neurosis of humanity as a whole, and one that Freud hopes we will outgrow.

The idea of God as a human projection is arguably one of the most characteristic ideas of the modern world. Some take this idea in the anti-religious direction of Freud and hope that, once the curtain has been pulled back, we will all see that the great and powerful Oz, is in fact, nothing but a creation of our own minds and we will finally be able to get over this God-thing once and for all. Since religion is an illusion, we would be well rid of it. Others, however, would acknowledge that our picture of God may be constructed from scraps of our personal and cultural histories, and that we don't really have any way of knowing how well, if at all, it corresponds with reality, but say that so long as our personal religious vision and values give meaning to our lives, we shouldn't try to get over them. We simply should make sure that we don't foist them off on others, who have their own personal religious visions and values. There may or may not be a reality lying behind those visions and values, but we can never get out of our own heads enough to gain access to that reality.

In this view, when we try to give an account of the ultimate meaning and purpose of our lives, it is a matter of human construction or projection. Perhaps because of the comprehensiveness of such ultimate beliefs they seem particularly unverifiable. We have no place to stand that is outside of our personal and communal histories. And it seems natural to us that when we seek to account for the ultimate meaning of our lives we would do so in terms of what we most value, which is usually an idealized version of our self: If we are white males, we think of God as a white male (but even more powerful). If we are a black woman, we think of God as a black woman. Presumably, if we were a platypus we would think of God as a platypus.

If we want to hang on to those ultimate accounts, we accept their projected character and retreat into the notion that (so long as they serve our needs and do no harm to others) their relation to reality is not particularly important, and perhaps even completely irrelevant. According to this perspective, the solution to the problem of religion as illusion is to think of religious beliefs as more or less benign coping mechanisms that we inherit from our families and cultures. Religion's value is practical. We construct a God who serves our purposes, to whom we can relate, with whom we can identify.

ARE WE GOD, OR NOT?

From the perspective of the Christian tradition—as well as the Jewish and Muslim traditions—there are problems with this solution, not least that it amounts to idolatry. It is calling something "God" that is, in fact, not God. In this way, Christians and Jews and Muslims agree with Freud: One ought not to worship an illusion, no matter how useful it is. In the Christian mystical tradition, this desire to worship the work of our own hands and minds has been viewed less as the violation of a divine commandment against idolatry and more as a deep spiritual problem that threatens our ultimate happiness by trapping us in the illusion of self-sufficiency.

The human ego has an immense gravitational pull. Left unchecked, it asserts its sovereignty by drawing everything into itself. The world becomes the world of *my* perception; the things I encounter are grasped in their relationship to *me*; the world is endowed by *me* with whatever truth it has; beauty is in the eye of the beholder, who is *me*. Even God cannot resist the ego's pull. Rather than being created in the image of God, I create God in *my* image. I make a God who serves *me*. I, in effect, take the place of God as the one who is the source of goodness, truth, and beauty.

But God is not harmed by our egoism; *we* are. Christianity's tradition of spiritual wisdom has long noted that an ego-centered existence subjects the self to stresses that it cannot long endure. We are quite simply an inappropriate center for the universe; we cannot bear the burden of endowing the world with its significance. The self does not possess sufficient meaning in itself to provide meaning for the world. A self that puts itself in the place of God finds itself not enriched but impoverished.

This is because we are not suited to be sources, but to be receptacles. We are not first givers, but receivers. Saint Paul wrote to the quarreling Christians at Corinth, "What do you have that you did not receive?" The shared faith of Jews, Christians, and Muslims in a God who creates the world in love and freedom amounts to a perception of all reality, including the ego, as a gift. Nothing except God is the source of its own existence, its own goodness, its own truth.

In terms of our relationship to God, this means that we are not the seekers, but the ones who are sought. In Luke's Gospel, Jesus tells numerous parables—of a woman searching for a lost coin, a shepherd searching for a lost sheep, a father running out to greet a lost son—that underscore this point. We do not initiate our relationship with God; the sheer fact of our existence means that we are always already standing in a relationship with God, a God who has sought us out of nothingness. And if God is already seeking us then perhaps we should not presume that the best that we can do is to construct our human ideas of God. Perhaps if we can loosen the ego's grasp on things we can move beyond the God of our illusions.

BESET BY ILLUSIONS

This is not to deny that we sometimes construct idols to worship. It is simply to say that our worship of those idols is not inevitable. If we allow it, we can relate to God and not simply to some idea we construct of God. But it is a tricky matter to distinguish between God and the very human conceptions by which we tend to understand God. Thomas Aquinas said that a thing is in the knower according to the mode of the knower, or, put more simply, the shape of the receptacle affects what is poured into it. Yes, a platypus would know God in a platypus-like way. But Aquinas also said that truth is the conformity of our mind to reality. While we may be beset by illusions and projections, it is possible to undergo what Freud called "education to reality"—though for Christians the reality to which they are educated is not Freud's world of impersonal forces but a world that finds its source in the freedom and love of God.

We might think of the Christian mystical tradition as a kind of education to reality. Such a claim would no doubt seem very strange to someone like Freud, for whom the visions and voices that are often taken to be at the heart of mysticism are prime examples of minds thoroughly beset by illusions. What could be more delusional than Catherine of Siena's belief that she had been given an invisible wedding ring by Christ, or Julian of Norwich's claim that she saw a crucifix bleeding? But whatever one may think of such phenomena, we should not take them as constituting the heart or focus of the teachings of Christian mystical writers. Rather, what they consistently return to are the various means by which we can overcome the illusions that beset us, so that the self may be freed from excessive self-centeredness so as to become more centered in God. This de-centering of the ego and centering in God frees us to see the reality that we have nothing that we have not received.

SILENT BEFORE GOD

One of the fundamental practices by which mystical theologians seek to be freed from illusion and educated to reality is what they call "detachment." No Christian writer has taken detachment in so radical a direction as the German Dominican Friar, Meister Eckhart. In the passage at the beginning of this chapter, taken from his "Counsels on Discernment," he makes the connection between being freed from the burden of interpreting all things in terms of ourselves and coming to a true knowledge of God.

He first notes that it is a mistake to think that we can possess God by means of constant mental exertion. Recognizing my illusions is not enough if I still think that it is up to *me* to overcome them. In trying to think ourselves out of idolatry we become a bit like the intrepid explorer in old Tarzan movies who falls into quicksand: The more we struggle to release ourselves the more deeply we become mired. We not only exhaust ourselves in the effort to produce an adequate conception of God, but we utterly fail in the effort. The best we can produce is an idol that is dependent on our efforts, not a source from which we receive. The achievements of our mental exertions with regard to God are, like all idols, bound to fail. Indeed, they are sterile at the outset; they *give* us nothing, but simply mirror ourselves back to us. As the prophet Habakkuk writes:

> What use is an idol once its maker has shaped it—
> a cast image, a teacher of lies?
> For its maker trusts in what has been made,
> though the product is only an idol that cannot speak!
> Alas for you who say to the wood, "Wake up!"
> to silent stone, "Rouse yourself!"
> Can it teach?
> See, it is gold and silver plated,
> and there is no breath in it at all
> (Habakkuk 2:18–19).

Like the Hebrew prophet, Eckhart recognizes the barrenness, the unfruitfulness, of the gods we construct: *"A man ought not to have a God who is just the product of his thought, nor should he be satisfied with that, because if the thought vanished, God too would vanish."* This is why Eckhart's understanding of detachment is so radical. We must not simply detach ourselves from excessive concern for worldly things, nor from selfish desires, but we must even detach ourselves from the god that we construct. This is the meaning of Eckhart's puzzling statement, "I pray to God that he may make me free of 'God.'" A god that we construct depends on us for its existence and has no "breath" (in Hebrew, *ruach*—"spirit") in it. If the god we possess is simply a product of our thought, a projection or construction, then such a god is as ephemeral as our thinking. Eckhart believes that such an idol should leave us profoundly unsatisfied. Unlike the God of

Genesis, who breathes "spirit" into Adam, the creature of mud, and makes him a living being, we must provide artificial respiration for the breathless idols that we construct, and the effort exhausts us; we simply cannot keep it up. It is *"impossible to nature to preserve such an intention, and very laborious"* because we are first and foremost not givers of breath and image, but receivers.

Therefore, we must still our minds and spirits so as to receive God's spirit, God's breath. This is why Habakkuk continues his critique of idolatry by reminding and exhorting us: "But the LORD is in his holy temple; let all the earth keep silence before him!"(Habakkuk 2:20). For ancient Israel, the Jerusalem temple was the dwelling place, the receptacle, of the LORD. And at the heart of the temple was the holy of holies, a chamber without images. The God of Israel prefers this dwelling to the pagan temples, well furnished with idols. The prophet calls upon the world to still *its* voice so that it can hear *God's* voice resounding in the emptiness of that imageless place.

So too for Eckhart, God dwells in the temple of the soul that is imageless, not the soul well furnished with concepts. It is by emptying the soul of its idols that we possess *"a God who is present."* God is not a distant entity that we must construct a conceptual ladder in order to reach, nor an absent figure that we hope to entice into us by decorating our soul with attractive ideas. For God is *"far above the notions of men and of all created things"* and dwells in us as pure gift, provided we do not *"willfully turn away from him."* And how do we avoid this? Not by any conceptual effort, but by detachment, which is simply "keeping silence before him."

Eckhart speaks often of the birth of the eternal Word of God in the soul. It is the silent soul that becomes the womb in which the true God can dwell.

DETACHMENT FROM WHAT?

There is a tendency in the Christian tradition not to see the radicalness of detachment, to think of detachment as detachment from particular things and circumstances. So we are told that we must not put our trust in riches or in friendship or in health, that all things except God are passing, so we had best not be attached to anything. This can become a kind of Christian stoicism that might have something to commend it as a coping strategy for the uncertainties of life, but that misses the deeper point of detachment.

Detachment is of no practical use. We do not detach ourselves from things because of the risk that they pose for us by their impermanence; we detach ourselves from them as a way of recognizing that we are not their source and they are not our destiny. Part of the burden that the ego places upon itself is the role of being the source of things and circumstances. "I must invest wisely in order to provide for my old age." "I must be accepting of an abusive friendship in order to preserve it." We must detach ourselves from these things so as to let them be what they are, which is what *God* judges them to be. And this allows us to let God be what *God* is, for in doing this, *"God forms himself for the man out of all things."*

Eckhart recognizes that we might think that the way to achieve "detachment" from *"the notions of men and of all created things"* is to remove ourselves from the world of created things. This is a temptation to be avoided, not least because it places God and God's world in a kind of competition with each other. While some Christian mystics *have* removed themselves to monasteries or cells or the tops of desert pillars, Eckhart does not think this is necessarily the best path. Indeed, the quest for physical solitude—physical detachment—can become itself another kind of idolatry. Eckhart himself led the active life of a teacher and preacher, not the contemplative life of a monk. The monastic life *may*, in fact, be the way for some to achieve detachment, but we cannot restrict detachment to monasteries. For Eckhart, detachment is the most fundamental virtue or character trait needed for a genuine relationship with God, therefore it must be able to be practiced in every situation and walk of life. The practice of detachment must be as omnipresent as God is. It is not for a spiritual elite.

So for someone who practices detachment, *"God shines in all things."* Notice, *God* shines, not *me*. The world is a reflection of *God*, not of *me*. Once the things of the world are freed from the gravitational pull of the ego they can become transparent to their true source: *"everything tastes . . . of God."* So detachment is not primarily from the things of this world, but from the self and its desire to be its own source by constructing its own god. Indeed, once our egos accept their fundamentally receptive nature, a new world is opened to us; detachment is not an impoverishing of our relationship to things, but an enrichment. We do not master the world with our ideas and concepts, but receive the world as God's gift, just as we receive ourselves as God's gift and even receive God as God's gift. For one who is truly detached, *"God's presence may shine out to him without any effort."*

Eckhart goes on to note that one *"cannot learn this by running away."* There may be good reason for taking up a life of *"external solitude,"* but we should not fool ourselves into thinking that it is a short-cut to detachment. Usually those who flee the world and its temptations find that they have brought the world with them. It was in the desert that Jesus was confronted with Satan's temptations. Therefore, we must learn to cultivate a *"a solitude of the spirit."* This is when the ego abandons all its props, not least of which is the illusion of its self-sufficiency, and clings to God as its sole source. Such solitude amounts to a radical trans-formation of our selves, a *"break through"* to the God who dwells in the temple of the soul without images, a breaking away from the ego's field of gravity so as to find God shining in all things.

FORGETTING OURSELVES ON PURPOSE

Eckhart stresses the effortlessness of detachment, while at the same time he says that the detached persons must *"acquire nakedness."* Now this is a strange notion. Is "nakedness" an acquisition? Isn't it rather a dispossession, a stripping? How does one acquire a dispossession?

There is a paradox at the heart of the Christian notion of detachment. The twentieth-century Trappist monk

Thomas Merton wrote that "we are invited to forget ourselves on purpose" so that we can "join in the general dance." This idea of forgetting ourselves on purpose captures the paradox and danger of spiritual disciplines. Precisely the conscious effort that we employ in self-forgetfulness can undermine that very forgetfulness. I focus so much time on self-denial that I don't have any time to focus on God. Or I try focusing on God so hard that I focus on myself focusing rather than on God. Yet without careful attention, and even exertion, how can I break through the pull of the ego? We need to cultivate practices of detachment, yet in doing so we run the risk of become attached to those practices.

How do we forget ourselves on purpose?

Eckhart's answer is that we must think of detachment as a kind of talent that must be cultivated. Anyone who has tried to learn a musical instrument knows that there is a difference between playing the instrument and playing the song. When one begins, one is so focused on the instrument that it is easy to lose any sense of the song that one is trying to play. With practice and the acquisition of skill, however, one can in a sense forget the instrument, and perhaps even forget the musician, and simply lose oneself in the song.

For someone who seeks to acquire detachment, *"at the beginning there must be attentiveness and a careful formation within himself, like a schoolboy setting himself to learn."* Given the deep-seated habits of the grasping ego, detachment is not something that just happens. It must be chosen and cultivated. But as we acquire the skill of detachment our focus can begin to shift from ourselves being detached to God. In the case of those whom the Christian tradition calls "saints," detachment becomes a "virtue," a second-nature that they do not need to consciously practice, but that has become—at least at times—like the beating of their pulse. The deepest truth about themselves, their receptivity, becomes the rhythm of their lives.

WHY ECKHART MATTERS NOW

But how do we cultivate the detachment that leads to this receptivity? This is something difficult to specify in advance, not least because we are all attached to different things and attached to our egos in different ways and will therefore require different forms of "education to reality." Eckhart himself is somewhat less than helpful, since he was very suspicious of any techniques that were designed to produce detachment. Certainly his emphasis on "interior" detachment over "exterior" technique can serve as a useful warning to us. But perhaps we can discern a few places to start.

A first step could be to recognize the deep hostility within ourselves to accepting the fact that we are not our own source. We need to recognize that we in the West live in a culture that values achievement and doing over simply existing. We need, at the outset, a careful self-scrutiny, examining the ways in which we seek to master and control the world. And we need to act intentionally to give up that control, precisely at those places where we seek to have it the most. Such a conscious scrutiny and renunciation of control would be what various writers call "purgation"—a stripping of idols from the temple of the soul.

The biggest idol that we need to remove may be the one that we have named "God," the god who comes and goes at my beck and call, the god who is a bigger and more powerful version of myself. This is why it is important to heed the advice of the prophet Habakkuk: Keep silence before God. Of course some have an understandable impulse to speak to God, to ask for what they need, or to thank God, or to lament and question. But arriving at silence before God is a crucial stop on the journey of detachment.

Once, some fifteen years ago, I made an eight-day silent retreat. I left on this retreat expecting much and was crushed when I discovered that I had carved out a week from my busy schedule for a meeting with God, and God seemed to have failed to show up. I prayed and meditated and read scripture and walked endlessly outdoors trying to appreciate the beauty of God's creation. But on this silent retreat it seemed that it was God who had decided to be silent.

I began to be really annoyed. Finally, after about six days, I was fed-up and told God to go to hell, that I could do just fine on my own.

Perhaps it was this recognition that what I had really been looking for was a god to serve my purposes that made the difference. Things began to change. Once I gave up on seeking God I was able to discover myself as sought. The emptiness of silence became the receptacle into which the Word of God was poured.

It is above all in those moments when one's voice runs out, when one gets tired of asking or thanking or lamenting or questioning, that a person can receive God's breath, so as to *be shaped through and through with the shape of the God he loves."*

Catherine of Siena
on *Love of God and Neighbor*

O eternal Father! O fiery abyss of charity! O eternal beauty, O eternal wisdom, O eternal goodness, O eternal mercy! O hope and refuge of sinners! O immeasurable generosity! O eternal, infinite Good! O mad lover! And you have need of your creature? It seems so to me, for you act as if you could not live without her, in spite of the fact that you are Life itself, and everything has life from you and nothing can have life without you. Why then are you so mad? Because you have fallen in love with what you have made! You are pleased and delighted over her within yourself, as if you were drunk [with desire] for her salvation. She runs away from you and you go looking for her. She strays and you draw closer to her. You clothed yourself in our humanity, and nearer than that you could not have come.

And what shall I say? I will stutter, "A-a," because there is nothing else I know how to say. Finite language cannot express the emotion of the soul who longs for you infinitely.

—Catherine of Siena (1347–1380)
The Dialogue §153

In a world of immense suffering, isn't the mystical cultivation of the inner life a morally dubious enterprise? Isn't mystical experience, at best, silent on the question of how we should relate to others, how we should address their needs? Isn't it, at worst, the height of self indulgence, a kind of spiritual autoeroticism in which one devotes oneself to the pleasures of "the flight of the alone to the alone" and is blinded to the needs of the world?

This attitude crops up not only among critics of religion, like Marx and Nietzsche, who see it as a "pie in the sky by and by" distraction from the pressing concerns of *this* life, but also among sincere religious people who, in practice if not in theory, treat other people as distractions that might draw them away from God. In his classic work, *The Imitation of Christ*, Thomas à Kempis quotes, with seeming approval, the Roman writer Seneca: "As often as I have been among men, I have returned home a lesser man." How can one possibly devote oneself to the inner life if one is constantly drawn away by worldly concerns? And even among those who do not want to separate the intense experience of God from concern for others, many wonder how they might properly integrate the love of God and the love of neighbor.

THE DEMANDS OF FAITH

For Christians, this question is of particular urgency. It is hardly a novelty in the Christian tradition to say that there is some sort of connection between loving God and loving other people. The prophets of the Old Testament constantly remind the people of Israel that they cannot simply fulfill their ritual obligations to God while ignoring their ethical obligations, particularly to the weak and defenseless. The prophet Micah famously summarized the demands of God: "He has told you, O mortal, what is good; and what does the LORD require of you but to do justice, and to love kindness, and to walk humbly with your God" (Micah 6:8). Jesus summed up and affirmed the faith of Israel: "'You shall love the Lord your God with all your heart, and with all your soul, and with all your mind.' This is the greatest and first commandment. And a second is like it: 'You shall love your neighbor as yourself'" (Matthew 22:37–39). The first letter of John says, "Those who say, 'I love God,' and hate their brothers or sisters, are liars; for those who do not love a brother or sister whom they have seen, cannot love God whom they have not seen. The commandment we have from him is this: those who love God must love their brothers and sisters also" (1 John 4:20–21).

Yet today there seems to be an even greater urgency to the imperative to link love of God to love of neighbor. Christians have renewed their awareness of the "horizontal" as well as the "vertical" dimensions of their faith and there is an increased sense that, in the words of the Second Vatican Council, "The joys and hopes, the sorrows and anxieties of people today, especially of those who are poor and afflicted, are also the joys and hopes, sorrows and anxieties of the disciples of Christ, and there is nothing truly human which does not also affect them" (*The Church in the Modern World* §1). Religious faith does not draw one away from the world, but more deeply into it.

It is not uncommon to find churches running emergency food pantries, homeless shelters, community centers, or providing space for various twelve-step programs. This increased Christian interest in and service to the world is no doubt frequently motivated by a healthy concern to live the message of Jesus in its fullness. But some motivations are not so healthy. With the decline in power and prestige of the churches, it may well be the case that Christians feel that they must demonstrate to the wider culture that Christianity is of some *practical* use, that Christians are good neighbors and can be good citizens. Indeed, many Christians understand social service to be as important, if not more important, than the more traditional activities of preaching and teaching and administering sacraments.

Perhaps people today seek to love God by loving their neighbor precisely because of the seeming disappearance of God from the modern world. As I noted earlier in discussing Thérèse of Lisieux, many modern people feel that they live in a world that is largely—even entirely—bereft of God. In such a world, the statement of 1 John that we cannot love God whom we have not seen acquires both poignancy and urgency: loving our neighbor seems the *only* path to loving God, since God seems to have vanished from our sight, eluded our grasp. But whatever the reason, the ethical component of Christianity has achieved a distinct prominence for many Christians today.

THE DEMANDS OF LOVE

Yet anyone who has tried to love their neighbor will recognize that this is a daunting task. In Dostoevsky's novel *The Brothers Karamazov,* the monk Father Zossima speaks with a wealthy woman who complains that, while she has a great love for humanity, she finds it difficult to love human beings because . . . well . . . the objects of her charity often seem so . . . ungrateful. Father Zossima replies, "Love in action is a harsh and dreadful thing compared with love in dreams." His words find an echo in my heart when I recall my own attempts to move love of neighbor from dream to action. For one thing, I find that many of my neighbors are either not interested in my love, or they are interested in it only for what they can get out of it, or they are interested in a sort of love that I am not interested in giving. In other words, my attempts at love of neighbor are met with either indifference or ingratitude.

It is tempting to think that the harshness and dreadfulness of love in action is a result of some sort of moral flaw in those we are trying to love. And certainly ingratitude and indifference are vices. But the real source of the difficulty we have in loving our neighbors in a concrete, active way is found not in them but in ourselves. Quite simply, we desire response and recognition; we yearn for our love to be reciprocated, appreciated, or at least acknowledged. This desire for response and recognition is not, however, a flaw— moral or otherwise. It is, in fact, simply an aspect of the fundamentally receptive nature of our existence that Eckhart's analysis of detachment revealed. Being a creature means that I am not my own source; I am by nature finite, limited, and dependent. In light of this, my neighbor's indifference or need becomes a threat to my limited self, the threat that I will be drained by my neighbor and receive nothing with which to replenish my self.

Today the demands of a harsh and dreadful love seem, if anything, to have grown greater. While modern technological advances have in many cases made it possible to alleviate our neighbor's suffering in ways previously unimaginable, they have also led to environmental devastation, increasingly deadly warfare, new moral quandaries about the beginnings and endings of life, and a growing gap between developed and underdeveloped nations. On a more general level, these technological advances have decreased our awareness of our fundamentally receptive natures. Our increasing technical mastery of hunger and disease can make us forget our limits, that not every situation can be mastered by us. Technological advance has heightened the expectation that every suffering can and *must* be alleviated.

We also suffer an increased awareness of the sheer scope of human need. Whereas in former times the answer to the question "Who is my neighbor?" could plausibly be restricted to those within one's immediate circle of acquaintance, our circle of acquaintance today has grown exponentially. Various media bring us into instant contact with hunger, disease, violence, and deprivation around the world. I have an instant and intimate image of swollen bellies and emaciated limbs, of bodies blasted by war and dying from AIDS. It is as if the whole world has become my neighbor and places a claim upon my love. Yet these new neighbors seem more unlikely than ever to recognize me or respond to my love. They come to me not in face-to-face encounter, but impersonally, over the television screen or through the mail or over the phone. I write them checks. They never write me back.

In light of such a clamor of voices demanding my love, and their non-response to my own voice, I am tempted to agree with Seneca that as often as I have been among people, I have returned home a lesser man. The demands of others chip away at my limited resources. As the world's need increases, I diminish. It seems at times that the only way to save myself is to retreat, to turn my back on and close my ears to the imperious demands of my many neighbors, to flee to the desert, or turn inward to cultivate my own spiritual garden. The "mystical" temptation sounds its call.

But is this really the temptation of the mystical tradition? When we look at different figures who are generally seen as part of the Christian "mystical" or "contemplative" tradition, we do not find the cultivation of a rich "inner" life to be a recoiling from the "exterior" world and its clamor of human need. We have already seen that for Ignatius, despite his emphasis on interior detachment from external circumstances, *all* things can serve the goal of honoring and praising God's glory; the inner life of prayer is inseparable from the exterior life of Christ-like activity. Similarly, Meister Eckhart reminded us that, for one who has achieved detachment, "God shines in all things" and that one cannot learn detachment by "running away."

Thus it seems that figures in the Christian mystical tradition do not necessarily pursue interior cultivation at the expense of love of neighbor. If this is the case, then how can the mystics help us in relating the love of God and the love of neighbor?

CONSUMED BY LOVE

Of those Christian writers commonly called mystics, perhaps none has written more profoundly on the theme of the love of neighbor than Catherine of Siena. Catherine Benincasa was the twenty-third of twenty-four children born to a well-to-do cloth dyer named Jacopo and his wife Lapa. In its own way, her life was as dramatic as that of Ignatius Loyola. After having at age seven what she would later describe as a vision of Christ, dressed in papal robes, enthroned above the church of San Domenico near her home, Catherine made a vow of virginity, as a way of consecrating her life to God. She kept this vow a secret, and as she grew up her parents made plans to arrange a suitable marriage for her. In order to forestall this event, Catherine cut off all her hair when she was fifteen, as a means of dissuading potential suitors. The next year she publicly announced her intention never to marry and in 1365, at the age of eighteen, Catherine received the habit of the *mantellate*, which was a group of women associated with the Dominican order who took vows of chastity and engaged is active works of charity, serving particularly the poor and the sick.

Rather than plunging into the typical work of the *mantellate*, as people expected, Catherine spent the next three years in isolation in her room in her family's home. During this period she learned to read (but not to write, which she would only learn later) and practiced severe penances such as extreme fasting, self-flagellation, keeping strict silence, etc. The only time she left her room was to go to Mass each day. This period of isolation culminated in what is known as Catherine's "mystical espousal" to Christ: an intense visionary experience in which she saw herself wedded to Christ.

Something about this experience led Catherine to leave her room and take up the *mantellate's* life of active service to those most in need. She engaged at first in the kinds of work that we today associate with a figure like Mother Teresa of Calcutta: tending to the most basic needs of the poor, the sick, and the dying. A circle of followers began to grow around Catherine, to whom she offered spiritual guidance and instruction, and who were present during her rather dramatic ecstasies and trances. In 1370 she underwent what has come to be called her "mystical death": For four hours Catherine seemed dead to all observers and upon her recovery of consciousness she claimed that she had in fact been dead, and seen heaven, hell, and purgatory. After this experience she widened her circle of activity, eventually becoming involved in the political conflict between the Pope and the city of Florence, as well as becoming one of the chief voices calling for the Pope to leave Avignon in southern France (where the papacy had resided under the thumb of the king of France since 1309) and return to Rome.

It was also in the early 1370s that Catherine became incapable of eating solid food, vomiting up anything she tried to consume, with the sole exception of the sacrament of the Eucharist. This affliction would remain with her for the rest of her life, and undoubtedly contributed to her early death. Yet, despite her growing weakness, Catherine continued to engage in vigorous activity, writing hundreds of letters, counseling her followers, and even traveling to Avignon in an ultimately successful attempt to persuade the Pope to return to Rome. She also composed her *Dialogue*, which, apart from her letters, constitutes her major spiritual writing. *The Dialogue*, which according to legend was dictated by Catherine while in a trance (though even if this is true, it is clear that she edited it later), takes the form of a rambling conversation between Catherine and God, in which God does most of the talking, covering topics ranging from creation to Christ to corruption in the Church.

Catherine died in 1379. Her last words were, "Oh Blood! Oh precious Blood!" And then, the words of Christ: "Lord, into thy hands I commend my spirit."

What should we make of such a life? What can such a person possibly teach us? Living as we do in a post-Freudian age, we cannot help but notice the erotic elements in Catherine's mysticism: her youthful vow of chastity, her mystical espousal. And living in an age in which young girls starve themselves in an attempt to control their lives, we cannot but see Catherine's extreme fasting as a form of *anorexia nervosa*. Does

Catherine of Siena's life confirm the suspicion that mysticism is a form of mental disease?

A couple points might be made here. First, some of what seems so bizarre to us in Catherine's life was not at all unusual in the Middle Ages. For example, virginity was a religious ideal that was held up for all, and it would not be unusual for even a young child to aspire to this (even before she fully understood what it was). Similarly, while a few eyebrows were no doubt raised in response to claims of "mystical espousal," many medieval writers saw the human experience of erotic love as a particularly rich source of language and images with which to express the intensity of one's desire for union with God. Such language was rooted in the *Song of Songs* in the Bible, a love poem that was seen by medieval theologians as an allegory of the soul's relationship with God.

I am sometimes amazed at how many of the students I teach, who live in a world where sex is used to sell everything from pop music to cars, are made extremely uncomfortable when a writer like Catherine speaks of her relationship to God in erotic tones. Perhaps this indicates a residual puritanism in them, or perhaps they fear that bringing sex into contact with God threatens to make sex a terribly serious matter, rather than the good clean fun that it is on television. In any case, medieval people thought sex *was* serious, and therefore the language of sex was a suitable way of speaking to and about God.

Second, other aspects of Catherine's life *were* manifestations of a kind of "sickness"—but this was something of which she was well aware. Catherine saw her inability to eat not as a form of extreme fasting, not as something that she willed herself to do, not as something under her control. She spoke with her confessor, Raymond of Capua, of "this infirmity which prevents me from taking food." While today we might diagnose her as suffering from something akin to the mental affliction *anorexia nervosa*, this should not necessarily make us dismiss her out of hand. What is important is how Catherine responded to this infirmity, this sickness. For Catherine, her inability to eat was not of itself of any spiritual significance. What was important was how she used her experience of suffering as a source of humility and compassion for her neighbors. Our sufferings (whether they be mental or physical) can become opportunities for uniting ourselves in solidarity with all the suffering people of the world.

SELF-KNOWLEDGE

The key to Catherine's thinking on love of neighbor—indeed the key to her thinking in general— is the need for us to dwell in what she calls "the cell of self knowledge." In using this phrase, Catherine is drawing on her own experience of three years of isolation in a room in her parents' house. Her room was her "cell"—the traditional name for the monk's room, which was his refuge of solitude. In the cell, one can focus one's thoughts and concentrate one's spiritual powers. In the cell, one was inescapably alone with God. To leave one's cell was, to many people's way of thinking, to place oneself in danger, to subject oneself to temptation. Again, we hear the warning voice of Seneca: "As often as I have been among men, I have returned home a lesser man."

For Catherine, however, what was crucial about the cell was the knowledge of God and self that confronts us when we are alone with God and have no distractions, no place, no activities, in which to hide. What we learn, as Catherine puts it to God in one of her prayers, is that "I am the one who is not, and you are the one who is." Or, as she puts it in the passage that stands at the head of this chapter: "*You are Life itself, and everything has life from you and nothing can have life without you.*" In other words, what is key for Catherine is the recognition, which we have seen already in Eckhart, that our natures are fundamentally receptive, and the correlative recognition that God's nature is radically generous.

Catherine does not see the poverty of the self as in any way threatening; for her it is the good news that we never encounter anything in the depths of ourselves but God's infinite love for us. To see ourselves as nothing is to see that our existence is the sign that God is a "*mad lover*"—one who loves beyond all reasonable bounds— who acts toward the creature "*as if you could not live without her, in spite of the fact that you are Life itself.*" Our nothingness shows us that God does not love us out of any need, but out of God's nature as "*immeasurable generosity,*" the "*fiery abyss of charity.*" Catherine believes that if we "dwell" in this knowledge, we receive a peace and security that goes far beyond what we can secure for ourselves through physical isolation.

One can dwell in the cell of self knowledge in all circumstances, which obviously allows for a life of active service to the neighbor. But Catherine's theology of the love of neighbor goes beyond this. Recall that it was at the end of her three years of isolation that Catherine emerged into active service of the poor and the sick: Something about knowing her own nothingness prompted her to a life of active service. For Catherine, prayer was not a respite from the strain and stress of a harsh and dreadful love; rather, it was the source from which that love flowed.

AS GOD LOVES

Catherine's development of the connection between self knowledge and love of neighbor has several facets. First, she recognizes that love normally involves a relationship of reciprocity; when someone loves us we desire to return that love. Yet if it is true that God creates out of *"immense generosity"* and not out of any need, what can I possibly give God in response? How does one give love to that which is the *"fiery abyss of charity?"*

God's gift to me of my existence is entirely free, entirely beyond anything I could demand, ask, imagine, or repay. Indeed, God loves me prior to my existence. Consequently, Catherine says, anything that I give to God is simply what is owed to God already, since everything I have and possess comes from God to begin with. In other words, we cannot love God with the same freedom and generosity with which God loves us because in loving God we are always motivated by the love that God has already given us; our love of God is in some sense always self interested, because God is the very ground of our selfhood. As God says to Catherine in *The Dialogue*:

> I ask you to love me with the same love
> with which I love you. But for me you can-
> not do this, for I loved you without being
> loved. Whatever love you have for me you
> owe me, so you love me not gratuitously
> but out of duty, while I love you not out of
> duty but gratuitously. So you cannot give
> me the kind of love I ask of you. This is
> why I have put you among your neighbors:
> so that you can do for them what you can-
> not do for me—that is, love them without
> any concern for thanks and without looking
> for any profit for yourself. And whatever
> you do for them I will consider done for me
> (Chapter 64).

Catherine's thinking here follows the logic of Jesus' saying in Matthew's Gospel about when Christ, the royal Son of Man, will return and pass his judgement upon the righteous:

> "I was hungry and you gave me food, I
> was thirsty and you gave me something to
> drink, I was a stranger and you welcomed
> me, I was naked and you gave me cloth-
> ing, I was sick and you took care of me, I
> was in prison and you visited me." Then
> the righteous will answer him, "Lord,
> when was it that we saw you hungry and
> gave you food, or thirsty and gave you

something to drink? And when was it that
we saw you a stranger and welcomed you,
or naked and gave you clothing? And
when was it that we saw you sick or in
prison and visited you?" And the king will
answer them, "Truly I tell you, just as you
did it to one of the least of these who are
members of my family, you did it to me"
(Matthew 25:35–40).

Love of neighbor solves the problem of reciprocity between divine and human love. We can love as God loves—that is, with nothing to gain from that loving—when we exercise that harsh and dreadful love for our neighbors who do not respond to or recognize our love. It is precisely in these acts of love that go unreciprocated that we most closely imitate God's own way of loving. Our gratuitous love of neighbor is accepted by God as gratuitous love of God.

THE SOURCE OF LOVE

Second, the knowledge that "I am the one who is not, and you are the one who is" means for Catherine that love is our most basic nature. In *The Dialogue* God says to Catherine: "The soul cannot live without love. She always wants to love something because love is the stuff she is made of" (Chapter 51). In other words, God brings the soul out of her nothingness entirely by an act of love; God loves the nonbeing into being. Thus if we think in terms of the "stuff" out of which the soul is made, we have divine love and . . . nothing.

The soul, therefore, cannot help but love. What keeps me from loving are those barriers traditionally known as "sin"—which for Catherine amounts to a perverse turning in upon the self, so that self-love usurps the love of God and neighbor. Catherine thinks that there is a proper place for self-love. But I only love myself properly when I am seeking above all else to love God by loving my neighbor. It is then that the self, whose nature is love, flourishes.

Catherine recognizes the harsh demands that love places upon us; she recognizes that the harsh and dreadful love of neighbor can seem to be more of a threat to the self rather than a means to the flourishing of the self. How do I keep the demands of love from draining me? In *The Dialogue* God speaks to Catherine using the image of a fountain:

> If you have received my love sincerely
> without self-interest, you will drink your
> neighbor's love sincerely. It is just like a
> vessel that you fill at the fountain. If you
> take it out of the fountain to drink, the
> vessel is soon empty. But if you hold your
> vessel in the fountain while you drink, it
> will not get empty: indeed, it will always be
> full (Chapter 64).

If I dwell within the cell of self-knowledge, keeping before me the truth that "I am the one who is not, and you are the one who is," then I remain connected to my self's true source. It is when I believe and behave as if I were my own source—when I sin—that I forget that love is the self's very nature and the demand of my neighbor becomes a threat.

WHY CATHERINE MATTERS NOW

Finally, for Catherine the ultimate model for human love is the foolishness of God's love displayed on the cross of Jesus. St. Paul says that "the message about the cross is foolishness to those who are perishing, but to us who are being saved it is the power of God" (1 Corinthians 1:18). The message of the cross empowers us for a radical love of our neighbor because it is in the cross that we truly see that God is a *"mad lover"* who acts *"as if you were drunk [with desire] for her salvation."* It is in the life and death of Jesus that we see the depths of God's love: *"She runs away from you and you go looking for her. She strays and you draw closer to her."* Above all, in the life of Jesus, Catherine sees the ultimate union of lover and beloved: *"You clothed yourself in our humanity, and nearer than that you could not have come."* The two become one flesh.

Catherine's own life reflects the foolishness of the cross. By most worldly measures of success, her attempts to put love into action were not terribly successful. Activities such as tending the sick and dying do not meet with long-term success: Everyone dies eventually. Catherine was a teacher and spiritual guide to many of her followers, but she died fairly young, with much of her promise unfulfilled. Even her success in persuading the Pope to return to Rome eventually led to a split in Western Christianity—with rival Popes in Rome and Avignon—that lasted nearly 40 years.

But worldly success is simply one more form of recognition and response that the love of neighbor so often denies us. For Catherine, true love of neighbor is always bereft of that sort of success. Ultimately, Christ-like love of neighbor will not satisfy the world's demands that Christianity be of some practical use. Rather, love of neighbor is a dialect of the language of prayer, one more attempt of finite creatures to speak to and about the infinite God. In the face of God's foolish love, Catherine asks, *"What shall I say? I will stutter, 'A-a,' because there is nothing else I know how to say. Finite language cannot express the emotion of the soul who longs for you infinitely."* Love of neighbor, with its failures and ambiguities and limitations, is the soul's stammering attempt to give expression to its desire for its infinite source.

Catherine's experience of God—her confrontation with the truth that "I am the one who is not, and you are the one who is" —inspired not passivity and self-cultivation, but rather demanded her stammering response of love. The demand of love is a harsh and dreadful one, as witnessed to by the cross of Jesus. But it is a demand that promises life, not death. This is because the demand of love is not first and foremost the demand of my neighbor, but the demand of God—a calling to the depths of my self by the one who is my source. It is a call to let myself be immersed in the fountain of God's love.

5 | How to be Green

Hildegard of Bingen
on Viriditas

Green
finger of God:
the vineyard you planted
glistens in heaven
like a pillar of light.
In preparing for God is your glory.

When he levels the mountains
you shall not be brought low,
O exalted one.
yet you stand afar off
like an exile,
though the armed man has no strength to seize you.

In preparing for God is your glory.
Glorify the Father,
the Spirit and the Son.
In preparing for God is your glory.

—Hildegard of Bingen (1098–1179)
Book of Divine Works

In asking why the mystics matter *now*, it seems that
again and again I have returned to the question of what
is distinctive about "now" and, again and again, I end
up making the point that what seems distinctive about
"now" is really a variation on some age-old theme

addressed by Christian mystics: belief and unbelief, the conflict between spirituality and service, and so on. It is true that some of these themes take on slightly different shadings today—the godlessness of the modern world is not the same as the godlessness of the biblical "fool" who has said in his heart that there is no God—but one might easily get the impression that all people at all times and places have confronted essentially the same fundamental issues. It begins to seem as if the writer of the book of Ecclesiastes is right: "What has been is what will be, and what has been done is what will be done; there is nothing new under the sun" (1:9).

But I don't think this is true. At least, not exactly. History is a place where things actually happen, and those things that happen are not simply manifestations of unchanging features of human existence but rather are occasions of genuine newness. What it means to be a twenty-first-century citizen of the post-industrial West is different from what it meant to be an twelfth-century citizen of European Christendom. At the same time, this newness is not *so* radical that the experience and wisdom of those who have come before us is simply irrelevant to these new situations. Otherwise, there would be little point in writing a book like this. So we must walk that fine line that acknowledges the genuine novelty of our situation (indeed, of *all* situations), while not dismissing what our ancestors have to teach us.

A NEW SENSE OF POWERLESSNESS

One of the genuinely new things confronting us today is what might be called "the environmental crisis." Since the second half of the nineteenth century we human beings have been using our nonrenewable resources and polluting our air and water at an unprecedented, and accelerating, rate. To take one example, the fossil fuels that currently provide 85 percent of the world's energy needs took millions of years to form. Even if we take seriously the optimistic claims of the oil and gas industry that technological advances will make previously unknown reserves available to us and will increase the efficiency of the engines that burn these fuels, it doesn't take a rocket scientist to figure out that we are using these resources much faster than they are being renewed, and that we will eventually run out. And in the meantime, the greenhouse gases produced by burning these fuels just might be raising the world's temperature (in the last 100 years the world's mean annual temperature has risen 1.3°F), which could result in everything from widespread drought to your cottage in the Adirondacks becoming beachfront property.

We could multiply the examples of genuinely new threats posed to the ecosystem in the past century and a half. The figures roar over us like a torrent: Eighty acres of rainforest disappear every minute; a quarter of the world's population is in imminent danger of chronic water shortages; up to one-fifth of the world's species could disappear in the next quarter century, almost entirely the result of human destruction of these species' habitats. And on and on.

This is something new, and it seems to call for a new way of thinking. Perhaps because most of our history has been a struggle against a natural world that was much more powerful than we were, we humans have tended to think of nature as something to be mastered—at times almost as an enemy to be conquered. If we did not keep our environment at bay, we would be destroyed. But now the tables seem to have turned. Now it seems that *we* are the threat. If we do not keep ourselves at bay, our environment will be destroyed.

In discussing the relationship between love of God and love of neighbor we saw how our increased awareness of the sheer quantity of human need—thanks to CNN, among others—can have a paralyzing effect upon us: What can *I* possibly do about all this human suffering and degradation? Similarly, the torrent of facts and figures about environmental degradation threatens to drown any resolve we might have to do anything about it. Despite bumper sticker slogans like "think globally, act locally," the scale and complexity of our ecosystem and its problems seem to make such local actions as recycling or carpooling appear ridiculously inadequate. Oddly enough, our sense of powerlessness before the power of nature has been replaced with a sense of powerlessness before the fragility of nature.

When human beings first began to gain a definitive ascendency over their environment—which we might, for convenience sake, associate with the "industrial revolution" of the eighteenth and nineteenth centuries—they assumed that nature was something like the giant steam engines that powered their new mills and propelled their new ships. Nature was a machine, which one could tinker with and fine tune in order to make it more efficient, more productive. And certainly nature could be "managed," much as one would manage a factory. However, the last fifty years has seen a growing awareness that our natural environment is nothing so simple as a steam engine or a factory. The interconnections between species, climate, and resources that make up our ecosystem are innumerable. It is less like a machine than it is like a body; its flourishing depends on a fine balance of factors.

Our awareness of this complexity can be a source of wonder or, just as easily, despair. In T. S. Eliot's poem "The Love Song of J. Alfred Prufrock" the speaker asks, "do I dare to eat a peach?" Today we might be more inclined to ask "do I dare to eat a banana?" Growing that banana has cost some number of square feet of rainforest, the pesticides used on it have helped poison the water, the workers who harvested it remain in poverty, and it has been brought to our local supermarket in a truck spewing forth greenhouse gasses. Do I dare to water my garden, drive my car, have another child? It is like a tiny thread hanging off of a sweater: It seems insignificant until we start to pull on it and before we know it the whole thing has unraveled. Is there any way to escape being complicit in the destruction of the environment?

A Thousand Questions

I suppose we could take this line of thought to the obvious conclusion: Just about anything we human beings do (except, perhaps, cleaning up toxic waste sites) has a negative impact on the planet. This is the view of the Voluntary Human Extinction Movement (VHMET— pronounced "vehement"), whose slogan, "Thank you for not breeding," sums up their solution to the problem: Since human beings are of no use to the rest of the ecosystem (not being a major source of food for any other animal, except maybe house pets) they should gradually phase themselves out by voluntarily choosing not to reproduce. Do I dare to have a child? No.

Whatever one thinks of the logic of VHMET's position, most people probably would like to think that something short of human extinction might do. There must be some point between strip mining and mass suicide that would allow us to preserve the environment *and* the human species. After all, we humans don't simply create waste. We also create symphonies and poems and cathedrals and that ought to count for something.

But the problem of in-between points is knowing where to locate them. *Do* I dare to eat a banana? How much time can I spend researching my food and its impact on the ecosystem? *Do* I dare to water my lawn? Can I really justify its verdant expanse, knowing as I do about the southward expansion of the Sahara desert? But does my little lawn *really* have that much impact on folks in Africa? Even if I water it, do I dare mow it with my power mower? *Do* I dare to drive a car? Should I rearrange my life so that I can walk or bike everywhere I need to go? But what about the pollutants that are created in the manufacture of my bike? Maybe I should just walk. But, when I walk to the grocery store, can I then buy produce that has been shipped in on trucks?

Do I dare to have a child? Can I really ask my child to forego such things as bananas and a green lawn to play on and travel by automobile to little league games played out of town? Do I tell her she can't have a bike because the steel from which it was made was refined with coal strip-mined from the hills of West Virginia?

We find ourselves with a thousand questions, a thousand excuses, and no idea of where to draw the line. Where can we look for guidance?

OUR PLACE IN NATURE

Traditional western religion does not seem a very promising place to look. Perhaps Buddhist notions of universal compassion or Jain practices of reverence for all life might be helpful, but certainly the Jewish and Christian God who says to the first man and woman, "Be fruitful and multiply, and fill the earth and subdue it" (Genesis 1:28) is just asking for environmental disaster. Aside from concerns about overpopulation raised by the command to fill the earth, the violence of the language of "subduing" the earth is chilling. Perhaps we might defang this particular command by putting it in context: It simply reflects a situation in which human beings lived in a threatening environment. Since the situation has changed, surely God no longer wants us to fill and subdue the earth.

But even if we render one verse harmless, have we really addressed the deeper problems of the Jewish and

Christian worldviews? Deeply embedded in those worldviews is the idea that human beings are somehow set apart from the rest of the world, that they occupy a special place in God's creation. In the first chapter of the book of Genesis, even though human beings are created along with the other land animals on the sixth day, their creation is singled out. Only human beings are created "in the image of God."

Advocates of what is called "deep ecology" see such ideas as being at the heart of the environmental crisis. According to Arne Naess, who is generally seen as the founder of the movement, one of the ultimate norms of deep ecology is "biocentric equality": the view that all living things have an equal and intrinsic worth and, therefore, an equal right to exist. It is precisely the view of human beings as standing apart from the rest of living things, as having greater worth, of having other living things at their disposal, that has led us to abuse our environment.

As an alternative or supplement to traditional religious views, some deep ecologists have put forward what is called the "Gaia Hypothesis," which says that all living beings on the earth are part of larger systems, which are in turn part of still larger systems, and that ultimately all of earth's life is part of a single living organism, called "Gaia" after an ancient Greek goddess of the earth. Our planet is alive not simply because it is populated by living organisms but because it itself is a living organism. Conceiving of "spirituality" as our relationship to something larger than ourselves, some have proposed that the something larger be Gaia—that super-organism of which we are part but which yet transcends us.

When we take the Gaia Hypothesis and make it the basis for a spirituality, we end up with something like pantheism—the view that "God" and "nature" are simply two words for the same thing. The radical immanence of God as nature means that God becomes, as William Wordsworth famously put it:

> A presence that disturbs me with the joy
> Of elevated thoughts; a sense sublime
> Of something far more deeply interfused,
> Whose dwelling is the light of setting suns,
> And the round ocean and the living air,
> And the blue sky, and in the mind of man:
> A motion and a spirit, that impels
> All thinking things, all objects of all thought,
> And rolls through all things.

NATURE'S PLACE IN GOD

It is difficult to read Wordsworth's "Lines Composed Above Tintern Abbey" and not feel the attraction of pantheism. Even apart from the sheer beauty of Wordsworth's language, there is the very attractive idea of an intimacy between human beings and God and nature, a common spirit or life force animating all things. In attending to the natural world, we are attending to God. And because we are thoroughly natural beings, we are at the same time divine.

However, there are also some problems with the pantheistic worldview. In particular, it can tend toward a naive view of the natural world. Along with Wordsworth's stirring lines, we ought also to recall Tennyson's description of nature as "red in tooth and claw." Despite Disney sentimentalities about the great circle of life, the natural world is a violent place, in which one being's flourishing often seems to depend on the destruction of another being. In nature, mutually beneficial cooperation sometimes seems the exception rather than the rule. The beauty of the lion masks the bloody carcasses of countless antelopes. Is this the world that we wish to identify with God? Is God also red in tooth and claw? Not surprisingly, many would wish to say no. For to identify God with the violence of nature would seem to indicate that this violence has the last word; it is what is most true about the world.

Whatever the merits and problems of pantheism, it is not the view that the Christian tradition, including the mystical tradition, takes on things. This, however, has not always been apparent. Both enthusiasts and critics of mysticism have sometimes identified it as a form of pantheism. Eckhart wrote, "The man who has God essentially present to him grasps God divinely, and to him God shines in all things; for everything tastes to him of God, and God forms himself for the man out of all things." A statement like this can plausibly be taken to imply that God quite simply *is* all things. However, what we have seen so far of the Christian mystical tradition is that it is almost the precise *opposite* of pantheism. There is a radical distinction between God and God's creation; God can be identified neither with any one creature nor with creation as a whole. For Eckhart, God shines in all things precisely because God—as the source of all being—exceeds and transcends all things. The immanence of God for the Christian mystic is not the immanence of pantheism, but the immanence of radical transcendence.

Does this mean that the mystics are of no help to us in thinking about how to live as part of our natural environment? Does the mystical understanding of the radical transcendence of God render the natural world at best uninteresting? Or are there resources among the writings of the mystics that can help us think about our place in nature and nature's place in God? Can the Christian mystical tradition help us appreciate the importance of the natural environment in the journey of the self to union with God?

THE PROPER BALANCE

In recent years there has been a growing interest in the remarkable body of work produced by a twelfth-century nun named Hildegard of Bingen (1098–1179). Hildegard wrote books on medicine, science, and theology, and composed music: indeed, some people today know her primarily through her music. She is unquestionably one of the most popular of the Christian mystics today.

But Hildegard is an unlikely candidate for such popularity. Her life from age eight on was lived amid the austerities of a Benedictine convent. She was very stubborn and could be quite harsh with those who opposed her. And she had visions (perhaps associated with migraines) that rival the book of Revelation in their startling imagery and phantasmagoric detail. She does not seem like someone most of us would want to spend a lot of time with.

And yet, there is something about Hildegard that people, both in our day and in hers, find compelling. Part of her attraction today is no doubt accounted for by the fact that she was a very feisty woman. Motivated by her conviction that she was God's prophet, bearing God's message, she escaped, even if only partially, the constraints that medieval culture placed on women. She dared to write and preach and counsel—activities from which women were normally excluded. But it is not only the fact *that* she wrote, but it is also *what* she wrote. Hildegard developed a theology that closely integrated God, human beings, and nature, while maintaining crucial distinctions between them. In her day, as in ours, this is no mean achievement.

Central to Hildegard's theology is her notion of *viriditas* or "greenness." The color green figures prominently in Hildegard's visions, but *viriditas* indicates more than mere color. It is vigor and fertility and health. Thus, in her medical writings she commends the healing power of certain plants on the basis of their *viriditas*. And *viriditas* is not simply a property of what we would normally think of as living things; it is also a property of such inanimate things as rocks. Emeralds in particular are endowed with healing powers because they are saturated with *viriditas* (thus their green color). The natural world is not, for Hildegard, simply inert matter, but is filled with life and power.

The difference between her approach to the environment and ours can be seen in her writings on medical matters. Hildegard's medical writings are not really something that you would want your family physician referring to in trying to cure your bronchitis. They are a mishmash of the views of ancient physicians (such as Galen), folk remedies, and Hildegard's own theories and observations; they are not a result of experimentation and laboratory trials. So, for the most part, we cannot take them seriously today as therapies for physical ailments. But what remains of interest in them are the dominant metaphors of balance and vigor. Disease is not a result of our bodies being attacked by things in an essentially hostile environment, but of an imbalance in ourselves and between us and nature: a lack of harmony, a loss of greenness. Healing is more a matter of restoring the proper balance than it is of eliminating enemies.

There is perhaps some wisdom for us here. For example, modern science seems often to undercut its own achievements as it attempts to eliminate the causes of disease. Insecticides lead to ever more resistant insects; antibiotics lead to ever more durable germs. *Viriditas* might be seen as Hildegard's way of saying that our environment is more than simply the sum of its parts. It is not something that we can disassemble in order to make it more efficient, or more hospitable. For Hildegard, the world still fit together like a vast organism, possessed of life, filled with greenness. In some ways, her view of the world is akin to the notion of "Gaia"—the world as a living being—though, as we shall see, without the pantheistic overtones.

AN INTIMATE ENERGY

When, in her responsory (the verses chanted after one of the readings in the daily round of prayers of the convent) for the feast of St. Disibod, Hildegard invokes the *"green finger of God,"* she is invoking not simply the vitality of nature, but she is also indicating that this vitality is a manifestation of God's activity in the world. The life that suffuses the world flows forth from God, who is "the highest and fiery power" and has "kindled every living spark" (*The Book of Divine Works*, 1, 2).

Despite her emphasis on the immanence of God, Hildegard is not a pantheist; she does not simply identify God with *viriditas*. While greenness has its source in God, it is not itself God. God is always "other" to the world. This does not mean, however, that God's relationship to nature is not an intimate one. Indeed, it is precisely God's "otherness" that makes the language of intimacy appropriate. It seems a bit odd to speak of my relationship to myself in terms of intimacy. It is the fact that two lovers remain distinct from one another that makes intimate encounter possible. Intimacy occurs when an act of love bridges the distance of otherness.

In a relationship between lovers, the love that flows through them, giving life to their intimacy, is like what Hildegard means when she speaks of *viriditas*. We might say that *viriditas* is God's love, energizing the world, making it living and fruitful. Nothing exists without *viriditas* because nothing exists without God loving it and wanting it to exist. And for Hildegard the universality of greenness shows us the universality of God's love: "There is nothing in creation that does not have some radiance—either greenness or seeds or flowers, or beauty—otherwise it would not be part of creation" (*The Book of Divine Works*, 4, 11).

CULTIVATING LOVE

In contrast to some of her contemporaries, Hildegard does not see nature as the enemy of human beings; she is convinced that even those things that might seem to us hostile—stinging bees and nettles, lightning strikes and snake bites—are all part of God's creation and therefore, perhaps in a way that we cannot see, good. And in contrast to some modern thought on the environment, Hildegard does not see human beings as enemies of nature. One of the most notable things about Hildegard's vision of the natural world is how inextricably human beings are woven into it.

A striking image of Hildegard's understanding of the place of the human being in the cosmos is offered in an illumination found in a medieval manuscript of her *Book of Divine Works*. This depicts creation as a giant wheel, entirely encircled by the fiery personified image of divine Love. Contained within the wheel is a human figure, whose limbs seem to form the spokes of the wheel, holding it together. The image is not unlike Leonardo da Vinci's famous sketch, *Vitruvian Man*, which shows a man within a circle in order to demonstrate the perfection of human proportions. Hildegard believed the cosmos in its totality to be perfectly proportioned and balanced, and she believed that human beings reflected that perfection, precisely as the part of the cosmos that was capable of mirroring the totality. She writes, "God placed man on earth as if he were an elegant stone that reflects any other creature that looks into it" (*The Book of the Rewards of Life*, 1, 83).

One thing is clear. Hildegard would not share the goals of VHEMT. She is unabashed in describing humanity as being above all other creatures and assigning the rest of creation the role of serving humanity. This may be troubling to us, since it seems that it is precisely such views that have led to such environmental destruction. However, it is important to remember that for Hildegard this did not grant human beings license to do whatever they wanted to with their environment. Rather, humanity has a divinely appointed task: to help other creatures to fulfill their destiny of giving glory to their transcendent source. Human beings have been placed by God above the rest of creation precisely so that creation might be drawn into greater intimacy with God. As the repeated verse of the responsory of St. Disibod puts it, *in preparing for God is your glory.*

One way that we might think about the role of human beings in relation to the rest of creation is through the metaphor of "cultivation." The role of humanity is that of gardener in God's creation. The greenness that so strikes Hildegard is not just the greenness of the forest, but the cultivated greenness of the vineyard. Indeed, she uses this image to speak of St. Disibod's foundation of the monastery where Hildegard first lived: "*the vineyard you planted glistens in heaven like a pillar of light."* Disibod serves as the *"green finger of God"* precisely in the activity of cultivation.

The cultivation Hildegard speaks of here is not simply the cultivation of the land—its transformation into fields productive of food. Certainly medieval monasteries often had spectacular success in transforming "wastelands" into arable fields. But for Hildegard such activities were at best secondary and at worst a distraction. In her view, the chief activity of the monastery is the cultivation of the soul, the transformation of the wasteland of our heart into a land productive of charity. Humans serve the rest of creation best by growing closer to God in love. If we fail to cultivate love of God, this is not simply bad news for us, but bad news for creation as a whole, since it is our task to draw creation with us into God's love.

Perhaps what is new about our situation *vis a vis* our environment is simply that we can see more vividly than ever the negative effect of human evil on our fellow creatures. For Hildegard it took a singular act of theological imagination to make a connection between such vices as greed, laziness, violence, and pride and the harm done to creation as a whole. Now, anyone who has eyes to see and ears to hear is aware of how our greed and laziness and violence and pride harms creation. Hildegard is eerily prophetic when she writes "the air vomits forth dirt because of the uncleanliness of men; it then brings unjust and unworthy moisture that destroys the greenness and fruit that ought to nourish people. . . . This is because men close their mouths to righteousness and to the other virtues so that they do not have to open their mouths and hearts to truth" (*The Book of the Rewards of Life*, 3, 34).

GUIDED BY VERDITAS

When St. Paul wrote that creation was in "bondage to decay" and that it was still "groaning in labor pains" awaiting redemption (Romans 8:21–22) he was reflecting the view that human beings turning away from God had brought harm to the cosmos as a whole and that human redemption was tied up with the redemption of the cosmos. Paul, however, rejected the notion that human beings could bring about their own redemption, or that of the cosmos; God is the one whom creation awaits, not us. At the same time, Paul emphasized that it was important for Christians to lead lives that manifest the goodness of God—that they, as Paul puts it, "walk . . . according to the Spirit" (Romans 8:4). Another way that we might say this is that we must live in such a way that the greening power of God guides us.

In Hildegard's monastic context, walking according to the Spirit was integrally related to asceticism—the austere practice of not indulging our capacity for sensual delight. One of the most important things Hildegard might teach us about our relationship to our environment is the importance of recovering asceticism. Some of what Hildegard writes about asceticism might strike us as extreme, a denial of innocent pleasures. But are our pleasures really so innocent? Do I dare to eat a banana? water my garden? drive my car? have another child? The practice of asceticism does *not* mean instantly answering no to each of these questions. It does mean that we must give up our sense of entitlement to these things so that we can begin to consider saying no, at least on occasion.

Asceticism is a matter of freeing ourselves from all those things we consider necessities in order that we can know where to draw the line. In the responsory for St. Disibod, Hildegard says, *"the armed man has no strength to seize you."* The ascetic life strengthens us to resist our most powerful enemy: our own compulsive consumption. Today's ascetic practices might look quite different from Hildegard's. It might be a matter of the kind of car we drive, or don't drive. It might mean not buying certain foods, or giving up the latest gadget. But as with Hildegard's asceticism, it will involve becoming conscious of our consumption, our place within God's creation, and the way in which our actions contribute to the groaning of creation.

WHY HILDEGARD MATTERS NOW

A final lesson we might learn from Hildegard is the provisional character of all that we seek to preserve. The prophet Isaiah speaks of the sky being rolled up like a scroll (Isaiah 34:4) and Hildegard very much shared the view that nature was not an end in itself and that ultimately all that was enduring was love of God. The responsory for St. Disibod praises the saint's holiness by saying, *"when he levels the mountains you shall not be brought low."* Long before scientists told us that our sun would one day burn out, Hildegard knew that the project of "saving the earth" was in some sense a futile one. One day the mountains will be leveled. One day earth's atmosphere will evaporate into space.

One day every species of plant and animal will be extinct. No amount of recycling will prevent this from happening. We do not need religious faith to tell us that the long-long-term outlook for the earth is not good.

But perhaps we do need something like religious faith to tell us that, despite its eventual extinction, the natural world is worth preserving because it is God's good creation and we are a part of it. Our care for creation does not spring from optimism about our success, but from our willingness to take up the task of being God's gardeners. In cultivating the world we make it beautiful, and in making it beautiful we are made beautiful, and in becoming beautiful we share in the eternal beauty of God. So we cultivate the garden of the world the same way we cultivate all our gardens: not with assurance, but in hope. We put the seed of creation—which includes ourselves—into the earth and it dies. What shall spring up in its place? For Hildegard, though the mountains will be leveled and every living thing will die, there is still hope for a new heaven and a new earth, a new life for which creation waits.

6 | How to be Blue

Julian of Norwich
on Weal and Woe

After this he showed a sovereign spiritual loving in my soul. I was filled full of an everlasting sureness that took hold of me in power without any dread. . . . Yet this lasted but a while; then I was changed, left to myself with all the heaviness and weariness of life—I was burdened with myself, so that I barely had patience to live. . . . But soon enough our blessed Lord once again gave me that comfort and rest of soul. . . . And then I was shown once again that pain of feeling; then the loving joy: now the one, and now the other, many times repeating—I suppose some twenty in all. . . .

This vision was shown to my understanding, that it is necessary for some souls to feel this way, sometimes in comfort and sometimes failing, left all alone to themselves. For God wants us to know that it is he who keeps us surely whether we be in woe or weal. And for the good of our soul we are sometimes left to ourselves, without sin being always the cause; for at this time I had not sinned, for it was all so sudden, yet I was still left to myself. Equally, I did not deserve to have received all these feelings of bliss.

When it pleases him, our Lord gives freely of himself, and then sometimes he suffers us to feel in woe. Yet both are one and the same love; for it is God's will that we hold ourselves in his comfort with all our might. For bliss will last without end while pain passes and will be brought to nothing for

*those who will be saved. And therefore it is not God's will
that we linger in feelings of pain by mourning and sorrowing
over them, yet we should swiftly pass them by, keeping ourselves in his endless love.*

—*Julian of Norwich (died circa 1423)*
A Revelation of Love

I have found myself repeatedly speaking of how the
difficulties of modern life can be overwhelming—of
how we drive ourselves crazy trying to give all the
areas of our lives their due, of how we are bombarded
by televised images of the suffering of others, of how
we can despair in the face of our negative impact on
our natural environment. Perhaps it is no wonder that
depression seems to have reached epidemic
proportions in our society. Estimates are that
depression affects nineteen million people a year in the
United States, with twenty percent of the population
suffering from depression at some point in their life. In
the year 1999 (prior to losing patent rights), Eli Lilly
and Company earned over 2.6 billion dollars on sales of
the anti-depressant Prozac. With the annual sales of all
anti-depressants totaling around forty billion dollars in
the U.S., and no signs of life getting any less complex,
depression seems to be a growth industry. While the
difficulties of modern life may be overwhelming, they
are at least good news for the pharmaceuticals industry.

But I suspect that it is fundamentally mistaken to
see the widespread depression of our times simply as a
problem of external circumstances, as if what we need
is to find a way to fix things—in our world, in our

personal lives—and then we could be happy and contented again. I suspect this is a mistaken view because depression is not so much a matter of being overwhelmed by this or that situation in life, rather it is a matter of being overwhelmed by the very task of being a self.

No Escape From the Self

In his *Confessions*, Augustine of Hippo writes movingly of the effect that the death of a friend had on him as a young man of twenty-one. At the time of his friend's death, Augustine was still over a decade away from his famous conversion to Christianity and, looking back on this event, the older Augustine sees in his reaction something of the difficulties of being a self in a limited and fragile world. He writes of his younger self, "I had become to myself a vast problem. . . . I found myself heavily weighed down by a sense of being tired of living and scared of dying." Augustine speaks of his own soul as a horrific object of which he is unable to rid himself: "I carried my lacerated and bloody soul when it was unwilling to be carried by me. I found no place where I could put it down. . . . I had become to myself a place of unhappiness in which I could not bear to be; but I could not escape from myself."

Augustine goes on to note that the passing of time "has remarkable effects on the mind. . . . Gradually it repaired me with delights such as I used to enjoy, and to them my grief yielded." One begins to suspect that the forty-five-year-old author of the *Confessions* judges his younger self's grief to be the foolish and theatrical symptom of the unbridled but ephemeral passions of a young man. Yet even as he hints at the shallowness of his earlier grief, Augustine conveys with great artistry the depth of the emotions as he felt them at the time. And the more we read, the more we are drawn into the claustrophobic space of Augustine's grieving self.

One of the things that is striking in his description is the way in which his world becomes compressed into the sphere of his own ego. He no longer lives in a world of others, but in the narrow world of himself: "I could not escape from myself." It is as if he became for himself a dark and intolerable prison from which he could not escape. He focuses so much on his own grief that his friend seems forgotten, or at best a bit player in a drama in which Augustine's lacerated heart has the starring role. His grief, his depression, begins to seem perversely self-indulgent; it is a manifestation of an exorbitant self-concern, which is at the same time a self-loathing.

It is also interesting that it is the death of a friend that touches off his grief. Of course grief is a perfectly natural response to a friend's death, but something more is going on in the extravagance of Augustine's mourning. He has become wrapped up in himself following an event that reminds him of just how limited, just how finite our human selves are. The self from which he cannot escape is, like all human selves, a terminal case, a self that will die.

Tired of Living, Scared of Dying

Today we might be inclined to be more understanding of the narcissistic coloring of a young person's grief. Especially, we would want to take account of the biological bases for many cases of depression; to be depressed is not necessarily a moral flaw. At the same time, Augustine's description of his depression following his friend's death offers us some valuable insights into what is going on in at least some instances of depression.

His description of how depression compresses the world within the narrow confines of the ego is echoed by Elizabeth Wurtzel in her memoir *Prozac Nation*. She speaks of depression as "a self-involvement that is so deep and intense that it means that the sufferer cannot get out of her own head long enough to see what real good, what genuine loveliness, there is in the world around her." The suffering of depression is certainly genuine suffering, but it is a suffering that receives its distinctive coloring from the problematic finite self that is its cause.

This is the reason why it is a suffering that is not subject to any easy solution. One of the problems with psychotherapeutic treatments of depression is that mere insight is usually not enough to dispel depression. I can realize that I am depressed because I am locked into a self that is a "vast problem," but knowing that doesn't change the self that I am. A major theme in Augustine's narrative of his conversion is the way in which recognition of the truth is not sufficient to release the self from its bondage. This insight again finds echo in Elizabeth Wurtzel's memoir: "You'll still cling to your destructive, debilitating habits because the emotional tie to them is strong—so much stronger than any dime-store insight you might come up with—

that the stupid things you do are really the only things you've got that keep you centered and connected. They are the only things about you that make you *you*."

So we cling to sadness, as Augustine says, "tired of living and scared of dying." But because we are finite, death ultimately wins. Either we feed on the "carrion comfort" of despair that seems the only food that can sustain us, and we kill the self quietly, by degrees, through various forms of destructive behavior, or we do it dramatically, all at once, through suicide.

Confronted with suicide, particularly the suicide of a young and healthy person, we may shake our heads and say something like, "it just doesn't make sense; she had so much to live for." But of course it *does* make sense. As Prince Hamlet knew, if one wishes to "take arms against a sea of troubles" when that sea is the abyss of the depressed self, then those arms must be turned against oneself. Indeed, suicide may seem like the last chance to take charge of one's life.

Studies show that men are less likely than women to admit to and seek treatment for depression, but they are four times more likely to successfully commit suicide. Perhaps the cultural ideal of the male who is never weak, who is in control of all situations, makes it more difficult to live with the recognition that one is irreparably wounded in the very center of one's identity. Suicide may simply be the application to the problematic self of our desire to fix things. When we realize that the problem is not with this or that external matter—the situation in the world or our relationship with others—but with our very selves, when we have eradicated all external problems, the only choice left is to eradicate the problematic self.

Or it may simply be that we grow weary of this life that afflicts us so; we finally can no longer carry our lacerated heart. We lay it down and breathe a sigh of relief.

WOE AND WEAL

What could a woman from fourteenth-century England possibly have to say that could help us living in the depressed twenty-first century? We don't know enough about the life of the woman who today is called Julian of Norwich to know whether she would even understand the modern phenomenon of depression. Indeed, we don't even know her real name; she is called "Julian" because during the last part of her life she lived in a small house, called an anchorhold, built beside St. Julian's Church in Norwich. But we do know a good deal about the times in which she lived, which the historian Barbara Tuchman characterized as "the calamitous fourteenth century." We know that England was involved in a protracted war with France; we know that the church was split between rival Popes; we know that the Black Death killed as much as half of Europe's population. These were certainly depressing times.

More significantly, we also know that Julian was aware of the problematic self that is the real root of depression. Julian wrote a book (a highly unusual act for a woman in late-medieval England) recounting sixteen "showings" or visions that she had in May of

1373, as she lay on what she and those around her thought was her deathbed. In these visions, the crucified Christ spoke to her and assured her, in the phrase later made famous by T. S. Eliot, that "all shall be well and all manner of thing shall be well." Julian receives this message with gladness, but also with puzzlement, because she is aware of "*all the heaviness and weariness of life.*" Indeed, at one point she speaks of life as a prison and a penance; one gets the sense that she knows, perhaps firsthand, the claustrophobia of depression. God may say that "all shall be well," but such a promise echoes hollowly from within the prison of the self.

In recounting her visionary experience, which lasted over the course of several days, Julian speaks of an experience in which she was overwhelmed by rapidly alternating feelings of well-being and despair, or, as she puts it, "weal and woe." Her description of her feelings of well-being convey almost a sense of invulnerability: "*I was filled full of an everlasting sureness.*" Yet far from being everlasting, this feeling is immediately followed by a drastically different one: "*I was . . . left to myself with all the heaviness and weariness of life.*" This is then followed again by a sense of well-being, and then again, "*I was shown . . . that pain of feeling; then the loving joy: now the one, and now the other, many times repeating.*"

Julian's description of "*that pain of feeling*" is striking. She speaks of being "*left to myself,*" which conveys a sense of abandonment, but also something deeper: "*I was burdened with myself, so that I barely had patience to live."* The image of the self as a burden echoes Augustine's "lacerated and bloody soul," which he must carry, "tired of living and scared of dying." It echoes the need to cling to destructive habits that Elizabeth Wurtzel speaks of, the sense that "they are the only things about you that make you *you."*

Julian is extremely reflective about her spiritual experiences; she never takes them at face value but rather constantly applies her intellect in order to make as much sense of them as she can. Thus when she says, *"This vision was shown to my understanding,"* she is indicating that this experience was one in which she was to grasp some truth. And the first truth that she grasps is that neither the feeling of exaltation nor the depths of depression has anything to do with her moral worth. While she recognizes that *"pain of feeling"* might sometimes be a consequence of our own bad actions, in this particular case, *"I had not sinned, for it was all so sudden, yet I was still left to myself."* The rapid alternation of states of weal and woe could not possibly have anything to do with either punishment or reward, since there was no time in between them for her to have done anything to merit either. Sometimes we are the cause of our own mental state, be it good or bad. But sometimes we are not. The real question is, how do we learn to live with both weal and woe?

WHERE DOES THIS COME FROM?

While Julian seeks to gain insight from her experience of weal and woe, this is not Elizabeth Wurtzel's "dime-store insight," the insight that promises to make the woe vanish. Indeed, part of

Julian's insight is that the alternation of weal and woe is an element of life that cannot be uprooted without uprooting life itself. No matter how hard we try to "fix" ourselves, no matter how good we try to be—eating well, exercising, going to our therapist, taking our Prozac—there is no way to absolutely insure that the darkness of depression will not fall on us. Julian is convinced that *"it is necessary for some souls to feel this way, sometimes in comfort and sometimes failing, left all alone to themselves."*

But why is this the case? Julian says that this is God's will: *"When it pleases him, our Lord gives freely of himself, and then sometimes he suffers us to feel in woe."* Yet this is an extremely troubling notion. How can the loving God in whom Julian believes subject her to such feelings? Doesn't this make God seem like an arbitrary tyrant who abuses our spirits for his own amusement? Even though she says, *"For the good of our soul we are sometimes left to ourselves,"* one must ask how the *"pain of feeling"* involved in this being *"left to ourselves"* could possibly be good for our soul.

In a certain sense, Julian thinks that "why" is the wrong question. The fact of the matter is, our life simply *is* a mixture of weal and woe. Since this is the case, Julian presumes that it must in some sense be God's will, because, as she says in one place, "nothing is done by chance or by coincidence, but all things by the foreseeing wisdom of God." The question "why" is simply a formula for frustration. The question we really need answered is not "Where does this come from?" but "Where is this leading?" How is the loving God in whom Julian places her faith using her experience of weal and woe for the good of her soul?

GOD'S DESIRE

Julian believes that our deepest spiritual affliction is our unwillingness to believe in the absolutely unmitigated goodness of God. One of Julian's favorite ways of speaking of the mystery of the Trinity is to speak of God as "all-mighty, all-wisdom, and all-love." Our problem, she says, is that "some of us believe that God is almighty and *may* do all, and that he is all-wisdom and *can* do all; but that he is all-love and *will* do all, there we stop short." God may be infinitely powerful, and God may even be infinitely wise, but could God really be infinitely loving? Isn't God chiefly concerned with punishing us for our wrongdoings and transgressions? Isn't this why I am so desperately unhappy?

In other words, we don't believe that God's love is comprehensive enough to overcome our unloveliness. God must be as horrified as we are at our lacerated and bloody souls; God must feel the same disgust that we do at our attachment to our destructive, debilitating habits. But one of Julian's insights is that our problematic selves are a problem for *us*, not for God. We hate our finitude; God has loved it into existence. And even in those cases where we do engage in evil actions, Julian says repeatedly that God looks upon the sinner with "ruth (i.e. mercy) and compassion," not with blame. It is not that God does not see the evil in the human race; it is rather that God sees that the chief victim of human evil is humanity itself. God desires to heal our evil, not to punish it.

So when we experience the constricting confines of ourselves, Julian says that God lets us experience this because *"God wants us to know that it is he who keeps us surely whether we be in woe or weal."* We can't know *why* some people never seem to feel what William Styron called the "darkness visible" of depression, but we can know that it is not because God loves them more or that they are somehow less finite or that they are somehow morally superior. We do not have windows onto the psyches of others, we cannot see their hidden sufferings, so to submit to obsessive thoughts of "Why me?" and "Why not her?" is one of the ways in which *"we linger in feelings of pain."*

WHERE IS THIS GOING?

Urging us to turn from the question "Where does this come from?" to the question "Where is this going?" Julian offers a deceptively simple answer to this question: God. This is because, in Julian's view, *all* things are leading to God, "out of whom we have all come, in whom we are all enclosed, into whom we shall all go." This can certainly sound hollow to someone in the depths of depression. When she says, *"bliss will last without end while pain passes and will be brought to nothing for those who will be saved,"* Julian can seem to be offering the rather unhelpful counsel that life may be tough here, but if you're good everything will be O.K. once you die and go to heaven. But is this the best way to understand what she is saying?

In some sense, Julian *is* in fact saying that the woes that afflict us will pass with this life, but the well-being that we experience is a foretaste of our eternal destiny.

God's love is endless. Or, put better, the love that is God is without beginning or end. Pain is a shadow on existence, but existence is fundamentally good. And the eternal existence that is God is eternally good. Yet Julian is not holding out hope of heaven as some sort of reward, or consolation prize, for this life's sufferings. A person suffering from depression would likely refuse such a reward, saying "it's just not worth it." But Julian is not outlining a system of rewards and punishments; she is expressing her fundamental conviction that joy is more basic to existence than pain.

This conviction is at the heart of everything that Julian has to say. If you can understand your own existence as coming from, rooted in, and headed toward the dazzling goodness that people call God, then you are inexorably drawn to share in Julian's conviction. But Julian never pretends that she is offering an easy answer. She recognizes that it is hard work, the hardest work of all, to believe that in weal and in woe we experience *"one and the same love."* But this "work" is not characterized by the kind of activity that we usually associate with work. It involves a kind of radical receptivity that Julian names compassion.

This emphasis on receptivity is something we have encountered before in thinkers like Eckhart or Catherine of Siena. The Latin word *passio* has a range of meanings, from "feeling" to "emotion" to "suffering," but all of those meanings share a sense that a passion is something that occurs to us, something that enters into our soul and that we must receive. In this sense, happiness or depression, weal or woe, are passions that befall us. So part of the work of believing that in weal and in woe we experience *"one and the same love"* is the work of recognizing weal and woe as passions.

But Julian does not speak just of passions, she speaks above all of *com-passion*, or "suffering-with." The work she calls us to is not the work of self-acceptance, but the work of receiving the passion of others. Like Catherine, Julian sees love of God and love of neighbor as inseparable. But she emphasizes not so much the active service of our neighbor (though she in no way denies the importance of this) as the sometimes harder work of sharing their passion, the things that befall them that they can do nothing about, except to receive them. Like St. Paul she exhorts us, "Rejoice with those who rejoice, weep with those who weep" (Romans 12:15).

In doing this work, Julian understands us to be imitating, even sharing in, the work of Jesus. For Julian, the passion of Jesus, his suffering on the cross, was an act of compassion, a sharing in the sufferings of all humanity. When we engage in such compassion, Christ is present in us. In receiving the sufferings of another, we receive Christ. And it is through this personal encounter that we can understand our own existence as coming from, rooted in, and headed toward the dazzling goodness of God, and we can come to share the conviction that joy is more basic to existence than pain.

TOWARD ANOTHER

Both Augustine and Wurtzel have described the self-involvement that accompanies depression. But while depression can make us very self-absorbed, the very experience of emotional suffering can also open within us a space to receive the suffering of others. What Julian's counsel of compassion offers us is a way to turn our capacity for suffering away from ourselves and toward another. Opening ourselves to the passion of others is a spiritual practice that can keep despair in check by turning the source of our self-involvement into a resource for involvement with another.

What this practice might involve can be seen in one of the few things we actually know about Julian's life. When, at some point after receiving her visions, Julian moved into the anchorhold at St. Julian's, this could have been the ultimate act of self-absorption, like a chronic depressive retreating into her room. But this is not what Julian was doing. Her anchorhold had a window that opened out onto the world. At this window, Julian would receive those who came to her for spiritual advice.

One of those who came was a woman named Margery Kempe, a prosperous member of the emerging middle class and the mother of fourteen. Unlike Julian, we know quite a lot about Margery, since she wrote a book giving an extensive, if somewhat jumbled, account of her life. In this book she unselfconsciously recounts her spiritual ups (including marriage to the godhead) and downs (among them, visions of priests exposing their genitals to her), as well as her own behavior (weeping, groaning, screaming) that many of her neighbors found disturbing. And she also recounts a visit to Norwich, to visit the anchoress "Dame Julian."

Margery's account of her visit to Julian is perhaps a bit self-serving, telling us how Julian praised her, but enough of it rings true to give us an idea of how Julian dealt with those who came to her seeking counsel. Julian gives Margery some sound advice about not automatically trusting visions (to which Margery was prone) and testing her spiritual experiences against the criterion of love of God and love of neighbor, noting that a true visitation of the Holy Spirit brings with it sorrow for sin, devotion, and compassion. But from Margery's account it is clear that what Julian did that was most important was that she *listened* to Margery; she took her feelings seriously. Margery's description of her dealings with other people indicate that she was not always received so kindly. Indeed, in reading her book one can easily understand why people grew tired of listening to her. But Julian listened, with compassion.

This is not to say that becoming a therapist is the answer to one's depression. Many of the helping professions are reputed to be filled with those who are trying to deal (or not deal) with their own problems. It seems to me clear that one who is seriously depressed ought to *see* a therapist, not to *be* one. Therapists have to deal, like the rest of us, with this life of weal and woe. But a depressed person, who is *un*able to deal with woe, is unlikely to be of much help in a professional capacity.

But compassion is not a profession or a career. It is a way of life that is to be constantly practiced and cultivated by everyone. There is no shortage of suffering in the world; the opportunities to be compassionate greet us at every turn. For someone suffering from serious depression, the practice of compassion will no doubt have to begin in very small ways, with very mundane acts that may well go unnoticed, but which bit by bit begin to nudge our own suffering out of the center of our psyches. Compassion allows us to acknowledge our own woes, but to *"swiftly pass them by, keeping ourselves in his endless love."*

WHY JULIAN MATTERS NOW

So in the end, what a woman from fourteenth-century England has to say to us living in the depressed twenty-first century is summed up in the word "compassion." Julian believes that we have hope for a better life after this one, a life in which weal and woe are not mixed together, a life of eternal bliss. But this hope is not the answer to woe, because it cannot drag us out of the pit of the self in which depression imprisons us. If anything, hope for a better life after this one, when prescribed as the antidote to melancholy, can make us focus on our selves even more and increase our desire to be rid of this life.

But compassion, planted by God in our hearts with the blunt tool of woe, turns us away from ourselves. Our lacerated heart remains, in a sense, lacerated. It cannot ever be healed in this world of weal and woe. But its wounds can be filled with something other than its own problematic self. The space of suffering that depression hollows out within us can be filled with the passion of another as we bear their burden. In compassion, that which is "weakest" in us, our capacity for suffering, becomes our greatest strength.

How to Live and How to Die

Thomas Merton

on Following a Path

My Lord God, I have no idea where I am going. I do not see the road ahead of me. I cannot know for certain where it will end. Nor do I really know myself, and the fact that I think that I am following your will does not mean that I am actually doing so. But I believe that the desire to please you does in fact please you. And I hope I have that desire in all that I am doing. I hope that I will never do anything apart from that desire. And I know that if I do this you will lead me by the right road though I may know nothing about it. Therefore will I trust you always though I may seem to be lost and in the shadow of death. I will not fear, for you are ever with me, and you will never leave me to face my perils alone.

—Thomas Merton (1915–1968)
Thoughts in Solitude

We sometimes say that something "is a matter of life and death." But, of course, this doesn't say much, since *everything* is a matter of life and death, and it is only by virtue of great effort that we can forget this. And this great effort of forgetting shows something peculiar about us as human beings: our capacity for self-deception, particularly with regard to our own mortality. In this final chapter I want to look at the matters of life and death that I take to be at the heart of our modern (and premodern and postmodern) dilemmas and see how the Christian mystical tradition might make a difference. Why do the mystics matter to those who are faced with matters of life and death?

The short answer is that mysticism is about "seeing" or, in more traditional terms, "contemplation." It is first and foremost about "seeing" the dazzling darkness out of which all things come and to which all things return, the transcendent source of existence that, as Thomas Aquinas put it, "people call God." It is a tradition that has a particular perspective on life: We are beings with an origin in an "other" who loves us even before we exist. It is also a tradition that has a particular perspective on death: It is ultimately only by entering into death that we can arrive at our origin in the one who loved us into being. We might say that contemplation is a matter of seeing from this perspective.

But contemplation is also a matter of seeing through illusion and idols to the truth. We have already seen how a thinker like Meister Eckhart is concerned that the God in whom we believe is not an idol created in our own image. But the mystical tradition is not only about seeing God, it is also about seeing all things by the light of this dazzling darkness. Mystical practice is not only about overcoming our illusions about God, it is also about showing us the illusions that we harbor about ourselves, about our lives and our deaths.

SELF DELUSION

In discussing Eckhart, I drew a comparison with Sigmund Freud and his criticism of religion as an illusion. But religion wasn't the only illusion that Freud was concerned with. Indeed, the pioneers of psychoanalysis (Freud and, in a very different way, Jung) are often credited with discovering the subconscious and the way in which our minds can be quite actively engaged on a subconscious level in doing something of which we are unaware on a conscious level. It is this mechanism that accounts for the human capacity for self-deception. Freud's famous analysis of slips of the tongue shows one example of how our own reasons for what we say and do are not always immediately apparent to us. We think that we know ourselves, but our very speech betrays our illusions.

But simply being aware of the human capacity for self-deception is no guarantee that one will not fall prey to it. And this seems to be particularly the case with those matters that Freud saw as at the heart of the two most fundamental human drives: sex (*eros*) and death (*thanatos*). While Freud's interest in the human sex drive is rather well known, his interest in the "death instinct," which he saw as the destructive counterpart to the essentially creative erotic impulse, is not. For my purposes, it is sufficient to say that it is part of the power of these drives that they often operate in a subtle—indeed subterranean—manner.

So subtle is our mechanism for self-deception that not even Freud could escape it. Around 1916, Freud first noticed a painful swelling in the roof of his mouth, which he claimed went away upon smoking some particularly good cigars. It was more than six years later that he finally went to a doctor to have this looked at. Though the doctor recognized it as a malignant tumor, he told Freud that it was a pre-cancerous tumor. Freud quite willingly, even eagerly, accepted this diagnosis, though he was in a position to doubt it. The tumor was not adequately treated at this stage, and eventually resulted in Freud's death in 1939. Though Freud eventually recognized the terminal nature of his condition, and even asked his physician to hasten his end with an overdose of morphine, what is striking is how long he delayed that recognition.

Some have speculated that Freud did not want to give up smoking cigars, to which he was quite addicted, and so was willing to engage in wishful thinking regarding his true condition. But perhaps the matter is more complex than simply not wanting to give up an unhealthy pleasure. Perhaps we see here the fundamental human desire to in some way evade that which is most certain about our lives: the fact that they will end. Perhaps this thought is so difficult to face that even a master of suspicion like Freud will find some way to believe otherwise.

UNRAVELING

But why would this be a difficult thought to face? Perhaps it is because death involves a massive "undoing" of the self. Death involves a "dispiriting" and decomposition of the body in which the fundamental structures of our lives as living beings breaks down. It severs us from those human ties—parenthood, friendship, vocation—that give us our identity. Our own death is unthinkable because it is unraveling of the "I" that thinks.

At the same time, death waits for us in every shadow. Particularly as we age, signs of death are all around us. In the death of friends we begin the severing of relationship that will become complete at our own death. In the biological process of aging, our cells die, they fail to properly replicate themselves, they simply wear themselves out. Our bodies lose their vigor, our muscles their tone, we can't remember which toothbrush is ours, our passions cool. Death is as inevitable as it is unthinkable.

And so we speak of "natural" death. Death is something that is simply a part of how we are put together biologically; our death is a feature of the kind of beings we are. Nothing about our makeup indicates that eventual death is any sort of deviation in functioning of our bodies. We don't die because something "goes wrong" with our bodies. It is simply a part of how they function.

Yet the unthinkableness of death indicates that in some sense death remains profoundly *un*natural to us. Those who too serenely accept death with stoic resignation somehow disquiet us. Their acceptance of death as natural strikes us as unnatural. As Dylan Thomas wrote to his father:

> Do not go gentle into that good night,
> Old age should burn and rave at close of day;
> Rage, rage against the dying of the light!

Once death is recognized, we don't want a passive acceptance of it; we want to see it resisted.

But what precisely is it that we seek from the dying? What are we asking them for when we want them to fight against death? We are not seeking something for them, but something for ourselves. We want an affirmation of life that will strengthen *us*. We want the dying to shield us from death, to interpose themselves as protectors between us and death, to fight death for us.

Death Awaits Us

But the dying do not always stand between us and death; indeed, death is so close that it seems no others can interpose themselves. Even before the light begins to die, before our bodies begin to fail, revealing the onset of our natural death, violent death waits for us. The fragility of life makes death a constant possibility in a way that other things are not. Realistically speaking, it is not possible that ten minutes from now I will suddenly become a millionaire or President of the United States or fall in love. Such things, even falling in love, do not happen without warning. But it is entirely possible that ten minutes from now I could be dead. I could have a stroke. I could walk into the street and be hit by a car. I could trip walking down the stairs.

Natural death frightens us because we can see signs of its arrival, in ourselves and others. But violent death, unexpected and unforeseeable death, defeats us with its very immediacy and invisibility. Psalm 90 prays, "teach us to number our days," but, number them as we might, chances are we will get the number wrong. Actuarial tables may tell me I have thirty more years, but the random accident that will kill me next week says something different. Indeed, the lurking presence of sudden death makes zero the safest number to choose. Yet this too seems unthinkable. Wouldn't a life lived in constant preparation for death not be life at all, but rather a living death? So it appears better simply not to think about it.

Death has, of course, been a problem at all times and in all places, and some form of the denial of death can probably be found in all cultures. But death is somehow different—experienced differently—in the modern world. On the one hand, we have medical and technological means to forestall death's encroachment that were unimaginable in previous ages. The development of these technologies require us to give sustained attention to the unthinkable reality of death. But what sort of attention does it require? Do we think about death as a kind of mechanical problem to be solved? If that is how we think about it, then we are not *really* thinking about death. We are not thinking about *our* death, the death whose breath we can feel on our neck if we turn our mind to it for only a second; we are thinking about something held at a safe distance and subjected to our scientific gaze.

The scientific gaze distances us from death, not only because it gives us a mask of objectivity with which to hide—even from ourselves—the terror that *my* death inspires, but also because it allows me to think that my objective distancing of death will somehow, some day, allow me to defeat death. Death is approached not only as a problem to be mastered, but as a problem that *will* be mastered.

Issues of control, of activity and passivity, have cropped up again and again throughout this book, and it is beginning to look like they are the heart of the matter. We have met our desire for control and its attendant difficulties at every turn: The seeming godlessness of the world is connected with the growing human aspiration to control the world; our desire to be in control hinders our openness and receptivity and leads to the construction of idols; growing human control over the natural environment has led to the degradation of that environment; one of the chief frustrations of depression is the inability to be in control of our own emotional state. And now death, which always defeats us, no matter what our plans. Perhaps death is unthinkable because it would force us to think of ourselves as ultimately, finally, completely without control.

THE ILLUSION OF MASTERY

The problem of death really is just an intensification of the problem of life. We want to treat life as a series of essentially technological problems: What sort of scrubbers will chemically remove the sulfur dioxide from the gases leaving our smokestacks? What sort of selective serotonin reuptake inhibitor (SSRI) will lift the cloud in my mind? But life is not a problem to be solved; it is an uncontrollable mystery into which we must enter in faith, hope, and love. This doesn't mean that we shouldn't put scrubbers on our smokestacks or take our SSRI's, but perhaps we shouldn't let these things lead us to overestimate the degree of our control. Until recently, death, as much as we sought to deny it, has always served to remind us of the limits of our control. Try is we might, life always slips from our controlling grasp.

But technology holds out a seductive promise: We are progressively gaining more and more control over our environment and ourselves, life is ever more malleable in our hands, and we are now poised on the verge of becoming absolute masters of our own destiny. This promise is seductive because it is what we want most, what we have always wanted most. The old story of Adam and Eve tells us of human beings, "in the beginning," reaching out for the tree of knowledge in order to "be like God, knowing good and evil" (Genesis 3:5). Like all seductions, we are promised something that is genuinely desirable, genuinely good. Because human beings are created in the image of God, it is entirely natural for us to want to be like God. But the seduction of the serpent, the seduction of technology, tells us that what makes us most godlike is control. It tells us that absolute mastery is the key to being like God.

If life is for us a problem of technical mastery rather than uncontrollable mystery, then it is only natural that death would become for us the ultimate technical problem, since death is simply life *in extremis*. But death can be approached as a technical problem in several different ways. We might seek a technical solution that would delay the arrival of death, and perhaps even keep it at bay indefinitely. Or we might, as Freud did when the arrival of death became unavoidable, seek a technical solution that will hasten death, so that we remain masters of it.

Questions of life and death have most recently presented themselves in the form of debates over how we should treat people at the end of their lives. Do people have a right to die? Do physicians have a right to assist them in dying? Do physicians have a *duty* to assist them in dying? Indeed, do some people in some circumstances have a *duty* to die? Such questions involve immensely complicated and emotional issues ranging from the economics of resource allocation to the redemptive value of suffering. And for many these issues are intensely personal, involving a parent or sibling or other beloved person.

I would not presume here to make policy recommendations regarding physician-assisted suicide, but I would like to suggest that the issue is not about death at all, but about life and our desire to master life through technology. We might ask, why has the issue raised itself in the form of a debate over *physician-assisted* suicide? Is it perhaps because physicians control the technologies of life and death? Is it because they have the technical expertise to hold death off or hasten its arrival? They are in control and by enlisting their assistance we too gain control.

This is not to deny that for many people facing death the question is often simply one of how much suffering they can or want to endure. They do not enter into deep reflection on questions of control or technology. Although death and suffering are matters that confront particular, individual human beings, our attitudes toward death and suffering—indeed our attitudes toward life itself—are very much shaped by the ethos of our culture. The practical shape of our everyday lives reinforces the message that what counts most is control. Is it simply an accident that a culture that values control so much would struggle with questions about the technological control of death? Doctors have been able to hasten death for centuries (even if they have not been able to hold it at bay); why is it now that the question of physician assisted suicide occupies us to such a degree?

Perhaps it is because we have reached a point where the dream of absolute control seems more possible than ever before. And in the face of such a possibility, it turns out that control ultimately matters to us more than life. A life in which we are not in control is not a life worth living, and if the only choice left to us is the choice of life or death, then choosing death is the only way of exercising control.

WHAT CAN I CONTROL?

But is it really a bad thing to recognize and exercise our control over our lives? Aren't I, in some sense, in control of my life, responsible for the choices I make and the overall shape of the life that results? I cannot simply throw up my hands and say, "I'm not in charge here." I make decisions all the time, some of them very small ("What should I eat for breakfast?"), some of them quite momentous ("Do you take this woman to be you wedded spouse?"). And these decisions have consequence for which I am responsible precisely because I have some sort of control over my life.

Death is too threatening for me to really acknowledge because it is ultimately *outside* my control. But it is no less threatening to acknowledge that in life I am in some sense responsible, that some things are *within* my control. Alongside the denial of death, we also find a denial of responsibility, which is ultimately a denial that the life I live is *my* life, the life for which I am accountable.

Again, as with the denial of death, such denial is understandable because it is unbearable to think that we have control, but not absolute control. I am in some sense responsible for being a good parent to my children, to show them love and patience and compassion, so that they might grow up to be loving and patient and compassionate people. But I cannot guarantee that this will happen. There are other factors controlling the outcome, not least of which is the responsibility my children bear for their own lives. Yet I cannot simply say that it does not matter how I act toward them as their father; indeed, in a sense how I act is the *only* thing that matters, because it is the only thing I can control. But the act of staring unflinchingly at this very real but very limited measure is almost unbearable.

If the dream of absolute mastery is an illusion, so too is the dream of our actions not having consequences for which we are responsible. Between the illusions of absolute mastery and absolute non-responsibility we find the uneasy, paradoxical space where real human beings dwell.

MERTON'S PATH

In the opening lines of *the Divine Comedy*, Dante writes, "Midway on our life's journey, I found myself in dark woods, the right road lost." Dante speaks of these dark woods as "tangled, rough, and savage" because they are the woods of our lives, which also are tangled, rough, and savage. This image of finding oneself lost on a road through dark and tangled woods captures well the paradox of our lives. By the time we achieve awareness of ourselves we are already on the road and, in a sense, we are already lost. It was the choices of others—parents, teachers—that set us on the road, but at a certain point, "midway in our life's journey," we suddenly recognize that we are following a path. We don't know when or where we began and we don't know where this path is leading. We have a sense that the "right road" is lost, but how do we know which path is the right one? The path we are on is the only one we see.

We encounter Dante's image of being on a road and feeling oneself lost in Thomas Merton's prayer, with which this chapter begins. Merton was a Trappist monk at the Abbey of Gethsemani in rural Kentucky. The title of his best-selling autobiography, *The Seven Storey Mountain* (1948), invokes Dante's image of Mount Purgatory, which the redeemed must ascend in order to reach paradise. But it is only with the luxury of autobiographical retrospect that Merton is able to see his path through life as the purgatorial ascent to paradise. In his autobiography he writes: "Free by nature, in the image of God, I was nevertheless the prisoner of my own violence and my own selfishness, in the image of the world into which I was born." Merton recognizes that the violence and selfishness that keeps him bound is *his* and no one else's, but at the same time he is no less a prisoner. Much of his autobiography recounts (in somewhat sanitized form) the first twenty-five years of his life, which were spent in restless wandering, trying to achieve a freedom that was beyond his grasp. When he wrote *The Seven Storey Mountain*, after seven years in the monastery, he seems to have felt that the journey had come to an end; he had found a home and he knew where he was.

However, as Merton matured as a monk he came to realize that the tangled, rough, and savage territory of our lives is not quite so easily navigated. He came to recognize a perpetual restlessness within himself that, even if he was restricted to his monastery in Kentucky, would not remain confined. He continued to explore new intellectual and spiritual pathways, pursuing interests in Buddhism and the anti-war and civil rights movements of the 1960s. Toward the very end of his life he was allowed to leave the monastery to attend a conference on monasticism in Bangkok in 1968 and it was there that he died, electrocuted when turning on a fan after stepping from the shower. An unplanned end to an unplanned life.

ACCEPTING OUR LOSTNESS
The bizarre death of Merton is a grim (and at the same time comic) reminder that death lurks as our

companion in every corner. But Merton himself needed no reminder of this. Ten years before his death he wrote, *"My Lord God, I have no idea where I am going. I do not see the road ahead of me. I cannot know for certain where it will end."* Certainly he could not have imagined that it would end in Thailand, stopped by a faulty electric fan.

But the beginning of this prayer is something more than simply a statement of fact. It is an admission, a confession, if you will. Merton sounds like a man who has been driving with his wife for two hours, resolutely insisting that he is not lost, and who now admits to his wife what she has known for the last hour and forty-five minutes: He is lost. And it is only with the confession of this lostness that he can begin to find the right path. So long as he insists that he has the situation under control, he is truly without hope.

This confession of lostness reaches deeper than a simple admission that he does not know the land around him. It moves on to acknowledge that he also does not know the land within: *"Nor do I really know myself, and the fact that I think that I am following your will does not mean that I am actually doing so."* My confession of lostness must reach to my own self-knowledge, because the denial of lostness is at heart a denial of my human condition. When I look at my own heart, I can be no more sure of myself than I can be of anything else. There too, the landscape is tangled, rough, and savage. I may be profoundly convinced that I am doing God's will, but the depth of my conviction is not indication that I am actually doing God's will. Many people have committed atrocities in the firm conviction that it was God's will. Do I really know myself if I think that I am somehow immune to such self-deception?

The fact is, my life is inevitably "path-like," which means that I can never rise up to an all-seeing, all controlling view of things. I see, as St. Paul put it, "through a glass, darkly" (1 Corinthians 13:12), and the recognition of this is the only possible way out of the maze of self-deception. We ought to note in Dante's phrase, "I found myself in a dark wood," what it is that he finds in the dark woods: himself. It is in the recognition of the darkness within and around me, that I discover who I am.

BELIEVING, HOPING, DESIRING

Do we simply stop at our confession of lostness? Do we throw up our hands and stop our journey, having recognized the hopelessness of ever locating ourselves on the path? To do so would be once again to flee the uneasy, paradoxical space between absolute control and irresponsibility. The goal is not to find a way out of this space, but to find a way within it.

Merton's prayer continues: *"But I believe that the desire to please you does in fact please you. And I hope I have that desire in all that I am doing. I hope that I will never do anything apart from that desire."* The prayer turns on three actions: believing, hoping, and desiring. We are not left with our confession of lostness; we are left with faith, hope, and love.

Desire is not so much my striving for God, as it is the space that God opens up in me, an infinite space that corresponds to God's own infinity. But God does not simply open this space; God fills it. The love that makes its home in us is God's own love. Yet this space is an infinite space, and so my knowledge can never encompass it. Knowing my own desire, my own love, is a matter of believing and hoping.

"And I know that if I do this you will lead me by the right road though I may know nothing about it." Here we move, ever so slightly, from believing and hoping to knowing. Finding myself in dark woods, the right road lost, I know that God will lead me, precisely through my not knowing. The emphasis here is on "I know that *you* will lead me, because I cannot lead myself." In confessing my lostness, I find the certain knowledge of faith and hope.

The certainty of faith and hope is a certainty so peculiar that I wonder if I should even use the word. It is not the certainty of knowing that you have grasped the truth, that you have figured out the right path. Merton's life as a monk was a highly structured one, with prayer at certain times throughout the day, restrictions on whom he could see and where he could go, even strict restriction on speaking. And when he was a young monk he thought, "this is the right path." But later in his life he came to see that no path set down in advance, no path found on someone's map, is the "right" path. The "right" path, the "certain" path, is whatever one God leads me on, and I cannot determine in advance what that will be.

The monastic structures in which Merton lived were important not because they were the path, but because they were practices by which Merton could be weaned away from his attachment to his own will. St. Benedict, the founder of Western monasticism, spoke of the monastery as a "school for the Lord's service." It is a place of learning, but learning of a peculiar kind. The Latin word for school, *schola*, can also mean "choir," and the process of learning to sing with others is a good example of the kind of learning we need in order to have faith and hope. In a choir, one must give up one's own musical agenda and allow oneself to be led, not simply by the director, but by the music itself, and by the musical strengths and weaknesses of those with whom one sings. And over time, certain things become second nature. Above all, the effort is not quite so great because one has grown slightly less attached to one's own will.

The certain knowledge of faith and hope is not the knowledge of the distant, technological gaze. It is not the knowledge of a piece of music that one can gain by reading the score. Indeed, metaphors of "seeing" fail us here. It is more like the certainty of a skilled craftsperson, a knowledge that is not gained through abstract reflection but through long practice. It is a knowledge that is in the hands and feet and tongue.

NEVER ALONE

As his prayer concludes, Merton addresses the heart of the matter: *"Therefore will I trust you always though I may seem to be lost and in the shadow of death. I will not fear, for you are ever with me, and you will never leave me to face my perils alone."*

To confess ourselves lost is to recognize that we are in the shadow of death. To surrender the illusion of absolute control is to awaken to the reality of that which most forcefully demonstrates our lack of control. I may manage death's arrival, seeking out the best technology to preserve my life or hasten its end, but in the end the arrival of death is unmanageable. We cannot see the path ahead because when we look ahead we can discern only the darkness of death.

Yet when we look in faith and hope we can see something else, something no less dark, but something that can be trusted. We see the "you" to whom Merton addresses his prayer, the God to whom he confesses his lostness. This is not a god that lifts me out of our world and gives me an all-seeing view of the journey ahead. Rather God, for Merton, is the one whom I trust while still in darkness. God is the one who is "ever with me," not only in the darkness, but as the darkness, for what ultimately makes my life incomprehensible to me is that, at its root, it is a gift given by the God that no human mind can grasp. God is dark to me because I cannot imagine one who would *"never leave me to face my perils alone."* The promise contained in that little word *never* is the promise of a love so vast that the mind cannot take it in. It is not the shadowy darkness of death, the darkness of light blocked, but the darkness of a light so vast that we are blinded, and so must trust that light to lead us on the path.

WHY MERTON MATTERS NOW

Merton is summing up the heart of the mystical tradition of Christianity. We began in darkness with

Thérèse and the night of faith, and we end with this same night of faith. Merton asks, in his own way, the same question as Thérèse: How can we walk when it is too dark to see? And what Merton and Thérèse and the others I have written about tell us is that we see best when we see our blindness; we walk most confidently by letting ourselves be led, by relinquishing our plans and programs, by living our lives as a gift received rather than a prize won.

This is hard for us. And while it is not uniquely hard for us modern people, it is perhaps hard in a unique way. Though our lives are no less pervaded by death, in contrast with other times we are more successful in hiding this from ourselves. While death is in some sense a curse—a profoundly unnatural affliction—it is in another sense a friend, because a life lived in awareness of death is a life lived in awareness of life's limits. If I know I will die I am less tempted to mistake myself for God. But our modern capacity to control death's schedule, if not forever delay its arrival, can tempt us to think we are titans astride a world that we control.

In contrast to this titanism, we have Merton's simple prayer: *"My Lord God, I have no idea where I am going."* But this is not simply a confession of lostness; it is a confession of faith. Merton cannot know where he is going not simply because he lacks the information. He cannot know where he is going because he is on a journey into God, who is beyond our knowing. His prayer is a naming of that destination that cannot be named, and at the same time an invitation to join him on the path of lostness, on the journey toward God.

But this is a journey that can only be taken by those who will die; it cannot be taken by titans. Physical death is important, because it is physical death that finally ushers us into the fullness of God's presence. But more important are all the "little deaths" that we die along the path of our life. These involve letting go of what we love in the hope that we will receive it back, transformed, just as we hope to receive our physical life back, somehow transformed.

So we return to the heart of the matter: seeing and receiving. We must learn how to see ourselves truly in order to live truly. And to know how to live is to know how to die, and to know how to die is to know how to receive. For it is in death that we finally see that our life was a gift.

CONCLUSION

Why do the mystics matter now? Ultimately, the mystics matter *now* for the same reason they have *always* mattered. I have tried to show how our perplexities as modern people open up a space in our lives in which we can hear these mystic voices. And certainly death opens the most vast space of all. But the mystics do not matter because they provide us with a coping mechanism for the modern world. They do not matter because they help us with our problems. They do not even matter because they can help us deal with death. They matter because they can help us see and receive the deep mystery that pervades the world. They matter because they can carry us into the depths of divine love.

Frederick Christian Bauerschmidt is associate professor of theology at Loyola College in Maryland. He received his Ph.D. in theology and ethics in 1996 from Duke University and his M.A.R. in 1989 from Yale Divinity School. He is the author of numerous essays, articles, and book reviews, and of *Julian of Norwich and the Mystical Body Politic of Christ* (The University of Notre Dame Press, 1999). He recently completed two years as director of the Loyola International Nachbar Huis in Leuven, Belgium. He and his wife Maureen are the parents of three children: Denis, Thomas, and Sophia.

More mystical wisdom . . .

God Hunger
Discovering The Mystic in All of Us
by John Kirvan
Explores our profound hunger for God through 50 challenging experiences for the soul, built around the core insights of ten great Western mystics such as Thomas Merton, C.S. Lewis, Rumi, and others.
ISBN: 1-893732-03-7 / 192 pages, $12.95

Raw Faith
Nurturing the Believer in All of Us
by John Kirvan
This companion to *God Hunger* explores the faith that is needed to live with an unknowable God, offering 50 meditations rooted in the wisdom of mystics such as Simone Weil, Blaise Pascal, Henri Nouwen, and others.
ISBN: 1-893732-18-5 / 192 pages, $12.95

Silent Hope
Living With the Mystery of God
by John Kirvan
The third volume in the *God Hunger* trilogy draws upon the wisdom of mystics, focuses on the life that begins when we surrender to the hunger for God that demands persistent hope, and offers readers the opportunity to explore their own struggle with the silence of God.
ISBN: 1-893732-41-X / 192 pages, $12.95

There Is A God, There Is No God
A Companion For the Journey of Unknowing
by John Kirvan
Writing for those already somewhat familiar with the mystical tradition, John Kirvan offers insight about the essence of the spiritual journey – the darkness and uncertainty that one embraces after abandoning the clear and certain path. Includes 25 meditations.
ISBN: 1-893732-69-X / 160 pages, $12.95

Prices & availability subject to change.

Available at your local bookstore, online retailers, and from
SORIN BOOKS at www.sorinbooks.com or 1-800-282-1865.

F0SO103000000